# REBOOT
# REBUILD
# RECONQUER

CHRISTINA IOANNIDIS

NICOLA WALTHER

ISBN: 978-0-9567666-4-9

In loving memory of Nilyan Elena Pérez, Christina's Mother, an international pianist and woman whose resilience, poise and serenity will always be an inspiration.

## ACKNOWLEDGMENTS

There are too many people to thank for their contributions to both of our lives and our careers. Our husbands Dave and Axel have been instrumental in being true feminists of our time and supporting us in our various pursuits. Dave in particular has been our go-to digital expert and built the website for this book. To Ruby, Corrina and Tara who helped with the first edit of our combined thoughts and our mentors, most of whom have written their thoughts in the endorsements section.

# REBOOT REBUILD RECONQUER

# ENDORSEMENTS

*'Christina has an amazing, insightful way of sharing her life lessons with us. This book will change the way we look at our careers and embrace the challenges which come our way. A must read for budding professionals and leaders in the making '.* Najam Khawaja, Founder & Chairman TPH DDB / RAPP MEA

*'Navigating turbulent waters is never easy and all too often we feel lost at Sea. This refreshing book uses real life experiences to help guide the reader through practical steps to face today's challenges.'* Dee Caffari MBE, The First female to sail single handed and non-stop around the world the 'wrong way' (against prevailing winds and currents)

*'I have been a fan and a follower of Christina and Nicola for more than a decade – they bring rigour, experience, insight and lashings of joy to the important topic of how to create a new chapter in a world of uncertainty. I wholeheartedly recommend this book!'* Eleanor Mills Founder Noon.org.uk

*'Christina is someone who truly inspires me, she has an unparalleled passion for seeing things working well and for giving people practical tools to find their way through challenging situations and turning them into positive opportunities. This refreshing book gives some great practical and insightful steps that individuals can take towards following their dreams and following a rewarding career.'* Dr. Debbie Stanford-Kristiansen, General Manager at Exhibition World Bahrain - presented by ASM Global

*'From personal experience, I know that Christina has an extraordinary passion for helping people make the most of themselves and for insightful advice on developing your life, career and mindset. A truly helpful book in an uncertain world for all.'* Rita Clifton CBE, Portfolio Board Chair and Global Brand Expert

*'Both these women have been forged in fire. Based on real life experience, the book is full of insights and practical advice on navigating through challenging situations. In a world where change is the only constant, this book is a must read for all.'* Jacqueline Rachelle Yee, Board Director and Money20/20 RiseUp Leader 2020

*'Nicola has an unparalleled passion for seeing things working well and for giving people practical tools to find their way through challenging situations'* Suneel Bakhshi, President & Chief Executive Officer, Mizuho International plc

# REBOOT REBUILD RECONQUER

*'At a time when many people and organisations are struggling with huge uncertainty and change, this book is an invaluable blueprint and guide through the steps that we must take to thrive. Christina and Nicola have overcome these challenges personally and have transformed their lives and careers. They speak with passion, integrity and a common sense that comes from their real life experience. '* Robert Baker CEO, Potentia Talent Consulting; Partner at Solon Advisory; Non-Exec Director at Spktral and Talupp.

*'If you are stuck in a rut, this book is for you, packed with insights and nuggets from two incredible women who have seen it, done it and who have binned the t-shirt! If it is one book you buy this year to transform and re-invigorate your career, this is it! Inspiring, practical and motivational – well done Christina and Nicola.'* Vanessa Vallely OBE, CEO, WeAreTheCity/WeAreTechWomen

*'"Personal resilience" has been a theme of mine - particularly following 9-11 where I worked in the WTC. What Nicola and Christina have brought to life in this book will give all of us tools for our future and those of our teams (family, friends, and colleagues). They communicate with passion, integrity and a common sense that comes from real life experience linked into the world we have just passed through - the pandemic. The book is full of insightful and practical advice on navigating your career in an uncertain world'* Emily Landis Walker, Landis & Co, Senior Strategic Advisor, 911 Commission, IMF

*'This book is right on the button! Addressing the most significant and challenging issues for businesses right now. Positively motivating business owners to thrive & embrace change - ultimately become 'chameleonic'. Sarah Cook,* CEO The Tribe

*'Full of insightful and practical advice on navigating your career in an uncertain world.'* Peter James Mason, MD, Head of Debt Capital Markets, EMEA, Barclays

*'There is a lot written about the theory of transformation and change but it is sometimes harder to imagine how it relates to 'someone like me' - this book bridges that gap - providing enough of the theory to give you confidence, but a dose of real life to help you understand how it might be relevant to you.'* Emma Boggis, Non Exec Director English Institute of Sport, Tandem&M, National Lottery Community Fund, The Yorkshire Regiment, The Boat Race Company Ltd, previously CEO Sport & Recreation Alliance and Cabinet Office

*'The key to conquering business, lies in first conquering oneself. In Reboot, Rebuild, Reconquer, Nicola and Christina find a fantastic blend of both personal and business transformation tips and tools, that demonstrates the interwoven nature of mindset and the reality of modern leadership.'* Olly Reid - Creator & Co Founder - HUM4NS

# CONTENTS

# REBOOT REBUILD RECONQUER

ABOUT US

## Who are these women? And why did they write this book?

*'Survival goes not necessarily to the most intelligent or the strongest of the species, but to the one that is the most adaptable to change.'* Brian Tracy

## A Warm Welcome to the Transformation Strategies: Reboot, Rebuild, Reconquer™!

Welcome to the post Covid-19 world, where we have all realised that the power of survival lies with adaptability. We are now living in a world that is based around individuals being able to be agile, transformative, to have what Christina calls the 'chameleonic culture' a mindset of evolution and change inside of them.

In this book, you will work through the process by which you can develop strategies to design and execute personal, corporate and team transformation through the 3-part Reboot, Rebuild, Reconquer™ model. These phases are not easy and require focus and dedication. we have developed these methodologies as a step-by-step framework so that you can fuel your own self-paced transformative projects or, even, career pivots.

By utilising the Reboot, Rebuild, Reconquer™ framework you will follow the steps of a multitude of professionals who we have been working with since 2008, when the shockwaves of the most recent financial crisis hit corporate employees with enormous magnitude.

## Disclaimer: Fear and Uncertainty Go with the Territory

While you work through this book, you will no doubt encounter moments where you doubt yourself, where you feel uncertainty. We will offer you guidance and encourage you to keep going. In our experience, having a support group will also help you, which is why we invite you to join the Thriving Transformation Tribe. You will find instructions on how to access this Tribe and the other material relating to this book at the end of Chapter 1.

You will be going through a lot of soul searching as we progress; trust us, this positive energy generated when you discover so much about yourself will help you when you feel rejected. However, by persisting, you will develop the skills of resilience to really help you grow and develop your life or career as you want it.

## Christina on why Managing Transformation is a Skillset

In 2010, I co-wrote a book with a fantastically powerful woman, Nicola Walther. This was actually part of my personal Rebooting and Rebuilding. The book was all about how to retain female talent. We wrote this in the aftermath of the financial crisis, where what my co-author and I realised is that we represent a typical cohort of corporate women who left the corporate world to become entrepreneurs. We saw a new reality emerging and noticed that larger corporations had been slow to adapt properly to what, in 2022, is now an accepted norm: People were no longer sticking to one career within one single corporation and the expectations from employees were increasingly high.

In the past, you were expected to work in one company and have a traditional career path where you would move up the career ladder and, if you were one of the lucky few, you would eventually progress into the Boardroom. The dotted line in the diagram below shows, you move into the Boardroom and then you might become a Non-Executive Director. This was a traditional career path for anyone who worked in corporations and who was interested in having career longevity. However, managing this career path in today's world (as we argued in our book) is not easy – employees take time out: some of us have children, some of us have caring responsibilities of elderly people, or some of us decide to take a sabbatical, which is the second line, the flexible model, as we called it. So, what you see here is a shift -from the traditional to the new career model.

## Traditional

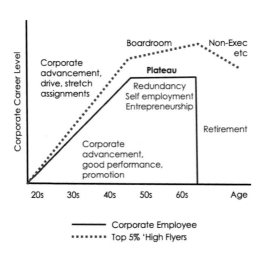

© Christina Ioannidis & Nicola Walther, 2010

## Flexible

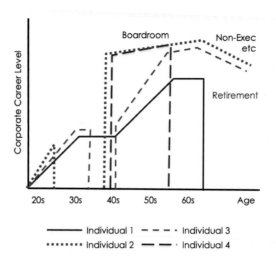

© Christina Ioannidis & Nicola Walther, 2010

Generation Z needs have supported what my co-author and I stated: The new corporate career path has to be a flexible model where individuals can go through different types of dialing in and dialing out of the corporate track, experiencing life, experiencing education or, even, entrepreneurship.

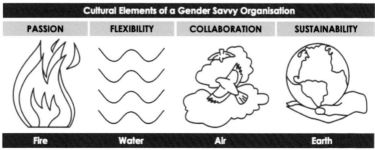

© Christina Ioannidis & Nicola Walther, 2010

Whilst this book is not focused on the gender angle, in the realities of Covid-19 many of us have actually fallen into one of these four flexible tracks, a lot of us have had to work in a different manner or have been made redundant, are looking for new opportunities or want to pivot our life altogether. So Covid-19 has actually increased the speed of transformation. The way in which we talk about the traditional careers being over also implies that as professionals or individuals we have to become intrinsically adaptable and able to navigate change, which is often anathema to us.

## *Fundamental Mistakes*

One of my strongest motivations for writing this book is that professionals mistakenly believe their work will 'do the talking for them' when considering a transition or transformation. I have also made that mistake. They, like I, are under a false illusion that people will remember them and their contribution when their company is restructuring or when they are made redundant. But, the reality is that people don't remember you, especially when times are hard, when times are difficult.

This is natural: when everyone is going through hardship, we all adhere to a survival instinct, where we retract, we retrench and focus on ourselves not on others. We look for opportunities for ourselves, not for somebody else.

*'Believing someone else is going to take care of you is really risky, and virtually never happens. As a (wo)man, I recommend that you should always be able to take care of yourself. If you are a mother (or father), make sure that you can take care of your kids because you can count on no one else but you. And that is a fact.'*
Emily Landis Walker

This is a quote from a very prominent US Financial Services veteran and consultant, Emily Landis Walker, and has always struck a chord with me. It is clear by what she states that you are your only anchor, no one else is going to take control of your career or give you the future you want.

You need to protect yourself; you need to build resilience internally, you need to come up with the strategies by which to grow and develop, this is why you are reading this book. You also know you are the person who is going to get you out of whatever situation you may be facing in your professional and personal realms.

And let's face it, you're probably in a tough place. Perhaps, even, facing depression. I appreciate that, and I suspect that fear and negativity are possibly knocking on your door at this very moment.

## Christina's Personal Story: From Corporate Highflyer to Potential Failure

I was always an over-achiever – I had been selected as Head Girl at school on the back of my excellent grades and personability. In my post-graduate studies, I earnt a Distinction in a Masters of Science in International Marketing. I was then selected to join an international graduate programme for the second largest spirits company in the world; from an international pool of 2500 applicants, I was one of the chosen 8. Thus began my corporate career, full of promise. I worked in Spain, Greece and London. I changed companies and industries multiple times, as I am someone who enjoys learning new things.

In the early 2000s, when the telecom bust ensued, I was made redundant twice in the space of 2 years. It seemed to be that I went from being on top of the world, having fantastic (and well-paid) jobs, to one day everything coming to a grinding halt... twice....

I was not prepared for this. I had never for one day or one moment actually thought that my dreams would come to a crashing halt twice in two years. I was in a rut. I felt like a loser. I was asking myself, 'why me'? What was it that had led me to experience redundancy twice in a row. Most people, at that time, did not experience it even once in their lifetime! Just after this happened, I had a tragic loss in my family. My grandmother, who was my inspiration in many ways, died. This threw me even more. And that is where my career took a bizarre turn – I decided at that point to launch an entrepreneurial venture. I had only worked in corporations before, so my mindset was one of working with large businesses; entrepreneurship was a very unknown territory to me. Yet, in 2003, I launched my first business: Aqua Studio, a business revolving around the design and commercialization of unique, bespoke jewellery. However, retail businesses are known to fail, and this is what happened for me. In 2007 I had to declare the company voluntarily insolvent and cease trading.

This hit me hard. I then went into a downward spiral, after a double redundancy, this happening within the space of 5 years it was a blow. However, I am, thankfully, a strong person, I was able to work through the whirlwind of emotions I was experiencing. No one guided me, no one supported me. Which is why I had to come up with my own strategies for transitioning my career, all of which are summarised in this book.

## Rebooting to Rebuild and Reconquer

My business failure was not in vain. On the contrary, when I launched this business, I realized that I am actually very creative and I love design, in every guise it takes. The ability to be creative gave me energy and immense feelings of positivity. So, when I lost the business, this realisation gave me the platform for my new life.

After my business loss, I spent a long time introspecting,

understanding what led to the loss of my business. I also spent time devouring books, trying to identify my next career move. It is the phase which was the most instructive to me, which is why I called it a Reboot. I was able to take stock of my failure, as well as my achievements. I built a picture of where I could go next using the new-found discovery of what gave me energy and made me happy. In essence, I discovered my passion and my purpose.

And my passion was this: changing mindsets and teaching others through my multitude of experiences and skills. I launched my second company - a training and consultancy business.  My first client was one of my former contacts from my (failed) jewellery business. And my co-author, Nicola, was also one of my former clients from that first venture. Both these women played such an instructive role in my transition, both supporting me with their friendship and in business. A critical part of the rebuilding process is identifying your MentoringMesh, your personal advisors who will help you open doors.

When times were more challenging and training contracts dry, I was able to also extend my reach in the interim consulting market, working within the growing sector of the online gaming industry. I was thus able to pivot from a traditional marketer to become a seasoned digital marketer, working in the growing areas of customer experience and customer relationship management. I worked with teams in blue chip companies such as Coral, Betfair, Ladbrokes plc. These experiences set me up for the next phase of consulting and training, as they added another string to my bow beyond diversity, leadership and marketing. As a result, I became a sought-after trainer, traveling all corners of the world and addressing audiences worldwide.

What I want to stress is that my multiple pivots did not take place overnight. They took commitment, dedication and a lot of strategic focus from my side. I had a vision of where I wanted to go, and I worked towards that vision. I have gone from living on 15 GBP a day as a budget after I lost my business, to being paid handsomely to travel to China, Singapore and many exotic locations to work. If I can do it, so can you.

All you need is to develop your inner 'chameleon' - your transformational mindset and use this as your guiding principle.

## Nicola on Vulnerability

Hello wonderful reader! It's my turn to give you some background and explain my part in all this. In my experience, people only take advice from the ones they feel they know, like and trust, so here's your chance to get to know a bit about me so you have a chance to like and trust what we are writing here.

When Christina asked me to write a second book with her, I was really excited. I knew that the things we wrote about in our previous book, over 10 years ago, were becoming increasingly relevant, and that the timing, post Covid-19, for a Reboot book was excellent.

I also remembered what a fantastic team we made. Both visionaries in our own way, we complement each other because I love organising, detail and finance, whereas Christina has a magnetic charm and a kind of magical skill set of drawing out the key issues and making sense of our ideas. She is also an intellectual with a curious mind who reads widely and deeply into her subject matter, for which I have a huge amount of respect; there is nothing shallow about this woman. I agreed to work with Christina's coaching material that she has developed over the years since our previous book. They are tried and tested modules and we just needed to write them up, consolidate a few things and add my own stories and diagrams. My side is usually to help with that last 20% of nitty gritty that I enjoy doing and Christina doesn't love so much! We even have a fledgling publishing company in my Hub with fantastic new talent willing to help us.

So why did I procrastinate in writing this for over two months? That's not like me at all. It was troubling me. Then, I went for a long walk with my good friend Maria. We go every Saturday morning, usually before the sun comes up, and we talk, a lot. We share everything about our lives. Maria is a fiery, intellectual woman and we share many similar trials and tribulations, which usually results in us falling about laughing on our walk. I was telling Maria about my procrastination on this book and what I was supposed to be writing about, and the penny finally dropped; I was not acknowledging the difference between showing vulnerability and being a victim.

Anyone who knows me will attest that I'm not shy about sharing what's going on in my life, so I know it's not a privacy thing. It dawned on me on this walk, I wasn't ready to write about this last 10 years because I still had an underlying concern about being painted as a victim.

Coaches will tell you, 'don't be in the drama triangle victim-hero-villain' otherwise you are going around in circles (or, in this case, triangles!). Now that's something I'd never want to accept in writing. Hey, I was raised to be STRONG, INDEPENDENT, RESILIENT and COURAGEOUS. And I AM all of these things, but that doesn't mean life has been straight forward and, if anything, I seek out those challenges that will allow me to grow. A smooth sea never made a strong sailor after all. That's why even when things are tough, I don't really see myself as a victim and it's difficult for me to be 'vulnerable' in sharing the trials of the past few years, not for privacy reasons, but that I genuinely see challenges as a blessing, become passionate about finding the lesson and try to help others in similar situations.

I've realised now that sharing these things actually doesn't paint me as a victim at all but being vulnerable with people can allow them to learn from your story and feel better about themselves. Don't get me wrong, I have yet to achieve any kind of Zen like mastery and I certainly do have a good moan about issues to my friends while I process a particular situation, but I really do believe everything comes along to help us grow and that is why this book is so important. I've listened to Tony Robbins since I was a child and he is still my favourite guru; my new ones include Mel Robbins, Brendan Burchard and Jeff Olson (if you haven't read *The Slight Edge* yet, add it to your reading list today!).

## *So what happened?*

My story since the last book involves an up and down entrepreneurial adventure coupled with some crippling medical issues and midlife challenges typical of many women in my 'sandwich' generation. When we wrote *Your Loss*, our second child had just been born and our family was living in London. I had a senior, employed, role in the City. Writing the book while on maternity leave gave me a great opportunity to re-evaluate what I wanted. I enjoyed the intellectual side of writing and working with Christina instilled me with a renewed passion for entrepreneurship.

My grandfather was an entrepreneur, as were several generations on that side of the family before him. It's in my blood. I had an idea for a banking product that might give people an opportunity to save a ton of money on their mortgages, so I left the bank and went about working with some awesome private equity guys to develop this product.

In the end, that didn't work out because we couldn't

convince the insurance regulators of its merits. In retrospect, that's because I didn't attend a key meeting as I was moving house to Bristol (the other side of the UK) that day. I should have had the confidence to rearrange the meeting and insist on going along. *That was a really big learning point for me.* Having come from a large corporate environment, I had to learn that *as an entrepreneur the buck always stops with you!* I made some decent money advising small businesses on derivatives during that time and I was surprised at how little these very successful entrepreneurs knew about banking products and finance.

My decision to leave the corporate banking world had given our family a lot more flexibility in terms of location. A job that seemed to meet all of my husband's criteria for his next step in his career came up in Bristol and he took it, thinking that it would give us a better lifestyle for raising our children. On moving to Bristol, my husband began working in a more senior role which was new and stressful for him.

Without really much discussion it was assumed that I would be responsible for settling the children and run the building project of a house we had taken on. Meanwhile, I was still picking up a few projects working with people from the City and selling our book, but my 'career' was not really discussed. I realise in hindsight that I was not emotionally ready to leave my home of 18 years, or my job that gave me a deep sense of fulfilment and self-worth. It doesn't mean it was necessarily the wrong decision for our family overall, but I skipped the inner work on what I really wanted to be doing and wasn't kind to myself about it, which left me over stressed and brought my relationships to breaking point.

What I did know at the time was that I didn't "fit in" here in this new city, the children were unhappy leaving their home, their cousins and all their friends, and we were living in a building site full of fleas. I volunteered at my University Boat Club as Treasurer and that kept me sane on many occasions. Having some real business issues to attend to that weren't building decisions, or the relentless overload of daily grind of household work, really helped. In a way, I guess that was my Mesh.

There's a whole other book about my health journey, which we will share in the next book because it ties in with many experiences we are hearing from women with whom we are working. For the sake of brevity here, I had some significant health issues, some avoidable had I known what I know now about the effects of cortisol on the body and the female hormones, and some not. I had a total of 7 operations, gained 25kgs (that's over 50lbs), and was on crutches for 9 months. It was seriously debilitating. This was the final straw and in 2013 I hit rock bottom in terms of my health and our marriage suffered. It has been a long road to recovery on every front and I'm grateful for some incredible friends and family who have been there through that particular journey.

Our building project was largely completed in 2015 and after a brief stint at an insurance company I realised it wasn't the right time to return to the corporate world. I needed and enjoyed the flexibility that entrepreneurs naturally have, and corporates have not yet figured out how to provide.

I began working again on a new entrepreneurial project. My business partner in that project and I took the idea to the Natwest Accelerator, an entrepreneurial incubator in the UK, where we had some fantastic support. I realised that my passion lay in developing strategy and financial plans with visionary entrepreneurs and helping them with those organisational areas they struggled with. Much as I did for my clients in banking and for my bosses when I was Chief of Staff and COO. In the bank where I worked for 15 years, they used to call it 'making the elephant dance'. I think what I do now is more like taming panthers, but it's a similar skillset!

When I was working in the NatWest Accelerator on what was essentially an engineering based project, we realised that we needed a flexible working space where we could bring our kit, only pay for the time we used and have meetings with various people. Having become more experienced in property, which had always been a passion of mine, we decided to buy an entire building and bring this idea of a high street based, co-working and event space to life. Meanwhile, we parked the original project so we could complete this one – something I'm really glad we did because I have learned that focus is super important.

Again, I learned some valuable lessons on that journey, which was made all the more challenging with Covid-19! Our financial situation became extremely challenging as development loans and associated rolled up interest outstripped the amount the banks were willing to lend in this climate. It has taken all of my financial knowledge, some outstanding, trusting and very patient business partners, and a husband who stepped up and took on the vast majority of the earnings over these two years to keep the ship afloat.

It has also taken a huge amount of deep healing for me personally to work through the emotional challenges that my medical issues threw up and to step back into my power as a business woman and a leader.

The Orange Tree Hub is now open and I'm excited to Rebuild my business there. I'm excited to return to my passion of growing businesses and sharing that growth with others.

With the combination of Christina's experience in developing a chameleonic, transformational mindset, and Nicola's resilience, we have much to share with you. This is why you are reading this book; so let's get started!

# CHAPTER 1
# THE GREAT REBOOT

*'Reinvent yourself, we are living at the time of the greatest change in all human history'* Brian Tracy

## Transformation is here to stay

TRANSFORMATION: A COVID-19 PREREQUISITE

Transformation is now a constant. We are required to change on an ongoing basis. During the Covid-19 pandemic, there has been no one left unscathed, and standing still has not been an option for anyone. Whether it's fighting the uncertainty of keeping your job or feeling the need for broader life change, we have all been affected.

In 2021, Microsoft research indicated that over 41% of employees were considering leaving their current employers in what has been called The Great Resignation[1]. The Covid-19 pandemic has had an unprecedented impact on all our lives, but the same research indicated that there are definite cohorts more greatly affected by the pandemic: working mothers, Generation Z and remote workers, for example. Whether you are in one of these categories or you are running a team with colleagues who fall into these categories, it is fundamental to be able to obtain the skillset to become 'chameleonic'. This is a word we use to describe an innate ability to transform yourself, your business, and those around you.

---

[1] Work Trend Index: 2021 Annual Report, 'Hybrid Work – Are We Ready?', March 2021

# REBOOT REBUILD RECONQUER

In this era of transformation, any leader, business-person or individual needs to build a tool-kit to achieve agility, flexibility and adaptability. In this book, you will discover the fundamentals of transformation. We will reveal how to overcome the natural, internal resistance that you are likely to face in order to thrive in a climate of change.

We, the authors of this book, are women who have been at the top of our game in business. We have been corporate highflyers with high paying jobs and responsibilities. Like most business-people, we were never taught the skills required to foster an attitude and capability for continuous change. We are typical of the generation we represent: successful business people who had to build the internal strength and power to transform themselves at the same time as juggling an increasingly complex set of responsibilities. We have to look after others as well as our own mental and physical health alongside our life-long career mission.

## THE FUNDAMENTALS OF TRANSFORMATION

In our multiple experiences of transformation (which we outlined in the previous chapter), successful transformation requires a three-step process.

- Phase One: Reboot

- Phase Two: Rebuild

- Phase Three: Reconquer

## PHASE ONE: REBOOT

The Reboot is the starting point: we need to review and reassess our life, our environment, our achievements. It is tempting to start by moving on, refusing to reappraise our past or review our life, but we always underestimate what we may have achieved, no matter our age.

In this book, we will spend a significant amount of time on this phase, working with you to help you recognize where you have come from and what you have attained in the past. If you ignore this step, you risk ignoring the signals of your past feats, endeavors and learnings. Whether your transformation relates to your life, your work, or your desire to get fit, it is important to know what has worked for you in the past and what you have learned from it, as well as what has not worked and what you should avoid.

In today's competitive world, leadership is associated with agility. Those who are the masters of their life have the ability to be introspective and leverage the power of their learnings (both good and bad) to shape their way forward.

Researcher and psychologist Carol Dweck espouses the power of the 'growth mindset' which she defines as: *'Based on the belief that your basic qualities are things you can cultivate through your efforts, your strategies, and help from others. Although people may differ in every which way — in their initial talents and aptitudes, interests, or temperaments — everyone can change and grow through application and experience...The passion for stretching yourself and sticking to it, even (or especially) when it's not going well, is the hallmark of the growth mindset. This is the mindset that allows people to thrive during some of the most challenging times in their lives'[2]*

---

[2] *Dweck, Carol. Mindset - Updated Edition: Changing The Way You think To Fulfil Your Potential. Page 12.*

# REBOOT REBUILD RECONQUER

We will give you our unique tools to build your growth mindset:

- Your Personal Achievements Log
- Your Life Milestone Graph
- Aligning your Strengths, Passions and Purpose
- Building Self-Worth - Quantifying your Achievements

Each one of these tools will give you a powerful rear-view picture of your life and career to date, helping you draw on learnings and experience, and sprinkling in the ability to grow your confidence.

PHASE TWO: REBUILD

Once you have completed the Reboot phase we will move into the rebuilding phase. The second phase is where you will really start shaping what your transformation will look like. The word transformation can itself be overwhelming and intimidating. We will overcome this hurdle by guiding you to consider what is it you want to achieve and why.

In fact, the question why is the most important and yet most seldom asked. For example, if you want to get fit, ask yourself why are you seeking this? Saying you want to get fit is not enough. Ask the question why again and you will start to identify the real motivations behind your desire to transform. For example, you may realise you want to get fit to 'look better'. Asking yourself a third time, you may reveal to yourself that your desire to get fit is a means to control your body. This technique of starting with 'why' and asking yourself the question multiple times is a well-known technique from neuro-linguistic programming which really helps us to identify our motivations. We would like to introduce this method into your day to day personal or business lives.

In phase 2, we also focus on generating control and allowing you to be the master of your own destiny. Very often, we feel like life just 'happens' to us; things occur and we feel we don't have any control over them. If we continue living this reality we are likely to fall into a victim mentality. We need to break the chain and understand that we are the captains of our own ships. We are our own anchor.

In this phase we will also start reshaping your future. We will redefine not only where we want to get to but how to get there, moving our resources (time, energy, investment) into high value areas - the areas where our finite resources can make the greatest impact. In doing this, we are making ourselves accountable as leaders of our life or business, setting parameters and holding ourselves responsible for pursuing our transformation. If we do not realise our individual responsibilities, we are likely to fall back into our normal mode of working and slip into the temptation of doing things just like we used to. Being a transformative leader requires ownership of each step and action in order to drive ourself or our teams forward.

Research has shown that once a person believes in a particular aspect of their identity, they are more likely to act in alignment with that belief[3]. In order to foster belief in your future identity, we will access the toolkit below:

- Building your BrandYou 2.0

- Creating your Brand Vision Board

To create these tools, we will use the power of visualisation to produce the agile future you. The entrepreneur and investor Naval Ravikant says, *'to write a*

---

[3] Clear, James, Atomic Habits, Page 34

*great book, you must first become the book.* [4] Like us, he is a firm believer in the importance of 'becoming' the transformation, of inhabiting the space and persona we aim to be.

As this process can seem unnatural, we will work through strategies for you to overcome the inevitable 'Impostor Syndrome', utilising the most effective reframing techniques for times of self-doubt.

PHASE THREE: RECONQUER

Whilst we are generally focused on working individually, transformation requires teamwork. It is impossible to take ownership of change all on your own. As the saying goes, 'it takes a village'. Whether your transformational project is personal or team-based, whether you are aiming to get fit, or you're preparing yourself to climb Mount Everest, people around you will be impacted by your decisions. They will also be a great source of support. So, you need to build the capability to take others with you on your journey, to encourage them to support you and to hopefully act as your greatest advocate too!

In the re-conquering phase, it is important to look at taking the right actions: the ways that you will stay on track, work through your doubts and be the new, fulfilled you. Very often we get to a point of achieving our aims but when our goal is reached, we revert to past behaviours. For example, when you get fit, you often find that within a short space of time your fitness decreases once more. This is why this phase is fundamental; you need to build a support system that will help you stay on track for the long haul.

At this point, you also have the responsibility to become a

---

[4] *quoted by Clear in Atomic Habits, Page 8*

role-model for change; to encourage those around to transform. Transformation is infectious: when you are on the right path, you automatically become more powerful and emanate strength. As a leader, it is important to build on this strength to help others. The reality is that if you can do it, anybody should be able to do it, and there is nothing more powerful than realising you have the ability to lead others on to the path you are treading.

In this phase we will bring together the concept of your Personal Capital (consisting of your brand, your personal contributions and your network, or Mentoring Mesh) and draw on the toolkits of:

- Building your Mentoring Mesh

- Redefining FEAR - with the FEAR antidote, the Personal Inspirations Pack

- Creating Environments which Embrace Change: Forming your Tribe and Mentoring Others.

We have worked with hundreds of individuals using these tried and tested techniques. We thank you for allowing us to guide you through your journey of transformation, a journey that you are likely to undertake a multitude of times in the Post Pandemic era. Let's get to it!

Reboot is all about getting back to what you are all about.

Rebuild what do you want next.

Reconquer ready for the next chapter!

# The RRR Model™

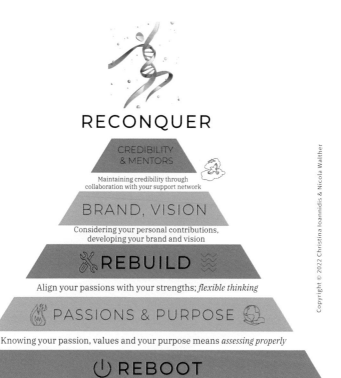

Throughout the book there are exercises and questions to answer. We encourage you to make your own notes, and the diagrams and exercises can be downloaded from our website: rebootmylife.guide

The password for downloading the worksheets is MyRRR.

# CHAPTER 2
# TRANSFORMATIONAL LEADERSHIP: FUNDAMENTALS

*'My mission in life is not merely to survive, but to thrive; and to do so with some passion, some compassion, some humor, and some style.'* Maya Angelou

## Why it starts with Passion

We believe that the heart of thriving transformation rests in achieving something which is meaningful to you, which will drive you forward in a new direction, which will bring out a brighter, more fulfilled 'you'. In this chapter, we will focus on the secrets of becoming the true you and identifying what makes you tick. We will explain why it all starts with passion and then move on to harnessing a positive energy to fuel your pivot or change.

In our research for our first book, *Your Loss: How to Win Back Your Female Talent*, the number one reason why women left corporations was because they felt creatively stifled and were not loving what they were doing. In other words, they had reached a plateau. The participants in our research identified that passion was the key to alter this.

This is why, when we developed our four-part model to reflect the cultural backdrop employees wanted addressed in order to stay in their organisation, passion was the starting point.  The complete model constitutes passion, flexibility, engagement and sustainability. We have since adapted this for the purposes of career, business and personal transformation, the themes of which make the backbone of this book.

Mark Antony, the famous Roman General, once said, *'If you do what you love, you'll never work a day in your life.'*

For some people, this may be a bit of a stereotype; but for us, the core of life is loving what you do.  You will find your personal transition goes a lot more smoothly when you focus on what makes your heart sing.

THE COMPETENCE TRAP

A lot of people fall into the trap, like we did, of doing something they are good at but which they don't enjoy. When this happens it is likely that you will become dissatisfied with your professional life, which also has an impact on your life in general.

We call this the Competence Trap. Why? We go through our life doing things we are competent in, but which do not mean anything to us, making us feel a malaise we cannot identify.  In Christina's late 20s, she was working in large companies in strategic marketing and strategy development with a lot of success. However, she felt extremely unhappy. As a single woman in the big city of London, she put the unhappiness down to that. In other words, she thought she was unhappy because she had not found a life partner. Fast-forward to her life as an entrepreneur, she realized that despite losing her business, she was completely happy with what she was doing. She came to the conclusion that what fueled her heart was using her innate creativity to positively impact others with powerful training programmes.

In our experience, a lot of people fall into the Competence Trap. They end up thinking of their day job as being on the 'treadmill'. living an existence which may pay the bills but does not fuel their emotional bank account.

How would you characterise your work? When you think about what you spend your days doing are you filled with dread or negative emotions? Or do you live your days able to do what you do with a sense of satisfaction?

## THE POWERFUL INTERSECTION: PASSION AND PURPOSE

You may have noticed that Christina's revelation, which reflected the original research for our book, also included an additional element: she discovered her purpose. So, even if you are not 'passionate' about something (and we do believe that everyone does have passion for something - but more of that in a bit...), your transformation will be more successful if you identify a purpose which is meaningful to you, that you work towards.

We have given you some headings in the diagram below. For example, what makes you feel free? What did you love as a child? Think about the things which get you out of bed in the morning. Think of the days when you know you have something in the diary where you really leap out of bed, the prospect of your day buzzing through your body. List anything that comes to mind, both in your work and leisure, such as tending to your garden, working on your car, writing a novel, travelling, etc. Focus on the moments when time has run away with you.

You can probably tell that one of Nicola's passions is creating beautiful graphics! When you have made your list, try to distill it to more than just tasks. So, if you write that you enjoy traveling, really pin-point what specific aspect of traveling you enjoy. Is it the excitement of being on an A380 aircraft (you are in awe of its engineering prowess), or is it the experience of new cultures, or the sampling of new cuisines?

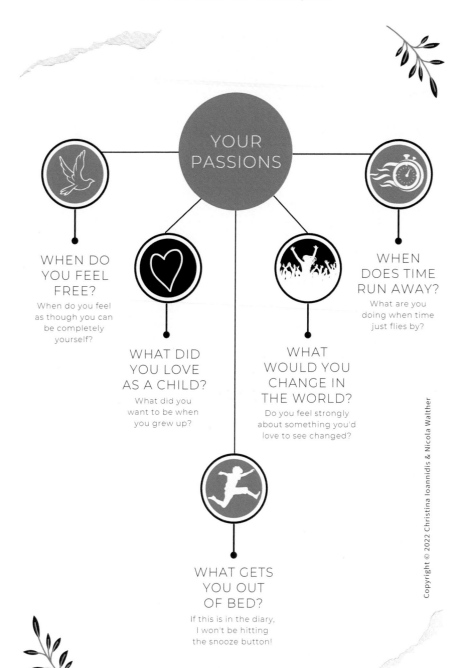

YOUR PASSIONS

**WHEN DO YOU FEEL FREE?**
When do you feel as though you can be completely yourself?

**WHAT DID YOU LOVE AS A CHILD?**
What did you want to be when you grew up?

**WHAT WOULD YOU CHANGE IN THE WORLD?**
Do you feel strongly about something you'd love to see changed?

**WHEN DOES TIME RUN AWAY?**
What are you doing when time just flies by?

**WHAT GETS YOU OUT OF BED?**
If this is in the diary, I won't be hitting the snooze button!

It may sound simplistic, but each one of the sub-examples on travel indicates different aspects of interest: a fascination in the A380 design could indicate an engineering interest; an interest in cross-cultural interactions could suggest a budding sociologist; a fascination in cooking and flavours could expose an inner chef in you.

And think as far back as your childhood. What were the things that made you happy then? What were the things that you really wanted to be when you were an adult? These may well give you indications of the things that you value and that contribute to your happiness. What would you add to your list?

Now review those activities which you have identified rock your boat. Can you identify any of these areas you can use your amazing skillsets and learnings (more about those in the next chapters) to make a difference to others?

Author and Wharton Professor Bea Boccalandro cites research undertaken with 5,000 employees over 5 years that uncovered that those employees with both purpose and passion place in the 80th percentile in performance, on average, per supervisor ratings. If you take passion away but still have purpose, average performance drops to the 64th percentile. If you take purpose away and are left with only passion, however, performance plummets to the 20th percentile.[5]

Here we would like to give you Christina's personal example: When she was about twelve or thirteen years old, her dream was to be an actress, with a specialisation for ancient Greek drama. She enjoyed giving emotionally

---

[5] https://www.wespire.com/the-difference-between-purpose-and-passion/

engaging performances and wished she could be some kind of performer. Her work today involving speaking and training is in many ways closely linked to performing: she's in front of an audience, imparting knowledge, on stage. She is still giving emotionally engaging performances because she seeks to inspire and make change in others. This is where her passion and purpose coincide.

Through her first and most significant pivot, Christina discovered that there are parallels between what she wanted to be when she was 13 years old and the turn her career would take. Do make sure you think about the parallels with what you used to enjoy when you were a child and what you wanted to 'do when you grew up'. Nicola says she never wants to grow up, but that she knows her passion is in starting businesses, personal growth, solving problems and providing space for people to grow their businesses. In her early childhood she started a puppet club and had a small business making paper fortune tellers, later teaching others how to make them. She reveled in seeing a playground full of those little paper games that she knew she had produced. She always loved being on or around water and she took those same passions into becoming an outstanding coxswain, coxing rowing eights, which she took up at University and still participates in as we write.

NICOLA'S PASSIONS

## WHAT DID YOU LOVE AS A CHILD?

I loved seeing other children play with the games I had made!

## WHAT GETS YOU OUT OF BED?

Getting out on the water steering rowing boats! I love the team atmosphere, the skill involved, the fresh air and the thought of winning races!

## THE SECRET SAUCE TO SUCCESS: LOGGING ACHIEVEMENTS

As humans, we tend to bury our achievements under the carpet. As we progress through our careers, and life in general, we seem to lose sight of what we have accomplished along the way. Ironically, what we do remember are the failures, hardships and difficult moments - we constantly leave ourselves open for criticism.

Yet the one thing which can be relied upon to build our confidence, is the act of remembering and honouring our achievements. Something magical happens when we recognise milestones in our past in which we have prevailed in some shape or form. This is why we encourage you to 'unbury' those achievements, to bring them to the forefront, to let them serve as an example of what we are capable of. They remind us that we can attain anything we put our minds to. Christina often has to practically pull achievements out of those coachees who attempt to inform her that they have never achieved anything in their life or career. They are now deeply grateful that she proved them wrong!

The issue with considering 'achievements' is that we tend to think of an 'achievement' as an extraordinary feat: be it climbing Mount Everest or winning an Olympic medal. However, an achievement doesn't necessarily have to fall into such a realm.  It just has to be something that you have completed that challenged and pushed you and of which you're very proud.

So, we invite you to list those achievements which are important to you. Think back all the way to your school days and then fast forward. Replay your life and take stock of those moments when you patted yourself on your back for having done something of which you are proud.

## GOOD AND BAD - IT ALL COUNTS!

In Christina's career, you might say that her first entrepreneurial venture, a jewellery shop, was not an achievement because it failed as a business. However, it is one of the achievements on her list. Why? She was able to commercialize it, make it happen, and push herself in a completely new direction revolving around creativity and design.

So, take some time to think about your life, your career, from the moment you started, to today. Log at least 10 achievements, and next to each write what you learnt from it. The learnings can be from either what are perceived as good or bad experiences. Whether you have shone at something or you have failed, it is all relevant. Both experiences are likely to have taught you something powerful.

When you have completed this, choose the top three of those achievements. Think of these three as the personal highlights of which you are most proud. As you go through this selection process, spend time thinking about what these top achievements indicate about your strengths and passions.

Returning to the example of Christina's first business, the retail outlet, she realized when doing this exercise that it is one of her greatest achievements. She is proud that she single-handedly created a new shop concept. She was also passionate about the industry as well as working with clients, so it was a win-win. This demonstrated to her that her strengths lie in designing and creating something new.  Nicola's first banking product never made it to market, but she discovered through the process how to raise equity, what to look for in business partners, and gained insight about leadership in the entrepreneurial space.

Do the same thing, look at your top three achievements and then look at what strengths they reveal in you. What strengths did you build on and develop as you worked through those achievements? Do those achievements relate to something that you are passionate about? Remember, the areas we achieve something in often reveal to us areas we could potentially thrive in!

Make sure to take a note of at least three things that you are passionate about. We hope your achievements build on what you are passionate about in the same way that the store did for Christina.

Once you've done this exercise, pause for a moment. You've now looked at your achievements and you've looked at what you're passionate about. In Christina's workshops, we look at our top three passions and ask ourselves, 'what are the professional opportunities that I can potentially gain in turning my passions into a business concept?'. If entrepreneurship is not an option for you, think, 'How can I include this activity as part of what I do in my working life?'

We had a woman who attended one of our workshops around passion and identified that one of her favorite things was horticulture and plants. She realised she was passionate about landscaping and making things grow. This woman had two options: She could either create a business around landscaping and horticulture, or she could include an element of sustainability in her work, e.g., green politics and growth as part of her transition back into the corporate world. This may not have been something she considered as part of her "career" until then, but when she did this exercise, she realised she could potentially create a business opportunity out of her passion in her time of 'reinvention'.

## INVEST THE TIME TO DISCOVER YOUR PASSION AND PURPOSE INTERSECTION

We encourage you to invest time on this chapter and in all of these exercises. You are now performing the most powerful of deep dives into your personal and professional trajectories. It takes time to reveal all the milestones that have meant something to you - which have taught as well as inspired you. This is a fundamental part of the rebooting process - taking that rearview mirror to your life and its tapestry of experiences which have been significant for you will be the stepping stone for your rebuilding and ultimate reconquering!

---

### BOX 1: FINDING THE INTERSECTION BETWEEN PASSION AND PURPOSE

What are your top 3 achievements?

- ...

- ...

- ...

Do they relate to something you are passionate about?

If you are unsure of your passions, what are the achievements revealing to you in terms of where you may be able to thrive in the future?

How can you use the activities which enthuse you to make a difference to others and drive your purpose?

---

# REBOOT REBUILD RECONQUER

# CHAPTER 3
# TO REBOOT...
# YOU NEED TO REASSESS

*'Your past shapes your future'* Christina Ioannidis

## Failures, Successes and Milestones

As professionals, we have realised it is possible to carry on our lives without focusing on the things that we have learned or the things that we have achieved. In addition, we seem to progress without being able to communicate those achievements and how they might be relevant in other industries.

In this chapter, we will look at how your professional past actually shapes your future, taking a deeper deep-dive into your professional successes and failures. All too often, we underestimate how much our failures can teach us.

THE LIFE MILESTONE GRAPH

This next exercise has its roots in Christina's personal Reboot. After she lost her first business, she sat down in a café and plotted out her career: from beginning to present day. What she realized in doing so is that when she had the complete career trajectory in front of her, she was able to really appreciate the different steps she had taken, and the milestones she had achieved along the way. Quite naturally, she started to write the learnings from each success and failure down, discovering that they were multiple. She realized how easy an exercise this was when she had the graph in front of her; The visual representation of her past.

Christina has run this exercise with her course delegates hundreds of times. Each person soon discovers how unique they are. There are no two people who have an identical Life Milestone Graph. Even if you have worked in one company all your life, there are no two individuals who would have had the exact same steps in their progression as you. This is all part of discovering what makes you the UNIQUE you.

---

### BOX 2: LIFE MILESTONE GRAPH

Take a sheet of paper and draw two axes. On the horizontal axis is time, and on the vertical access, is your life trajectory.

**PART 1** In the bottom left, begin with the start of your adult life - this could be at the end of your secondary education, at college, or whenever you are considered to have had your first relevant experiences. Draw a line upwards to indicate the upwards movements as you progressed in time in your life and positive progress; you can include downward trajectories to mark any challenging times, a failure or any point of negativity. As you shift projects or make job changes, things may recover again and your trajectory assumes an upward movement once more. It is important here not to get hung up on why you may feel something was a negative experience or moment. Just draw the line in the direction that comes naturally to you. Keep going until you arrive at where you are today.

**PART 2** For the second part of this exercise, go back and mark on the graph the key moments or milestones, good or bad, which were important to you. Do this up to the present day.

**PART 3** For the third part of this exercise, go back to each Milestone that you highlighted, and write under each what your main learnings were.

---

## PERSONAL SUCCESSES AND FAILURES: WHAT WERE THE GREATEST LEARNINGS?

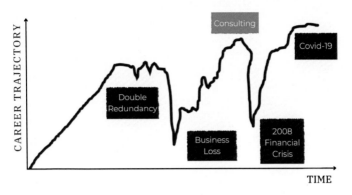

**Soft Skills:** Communication, Sales, Crisis Management, Leadership, Resilience
**Hard Skills:** Business Management, Digital Marketing

This is Christina's personal Life Milestone Graph and it is a fantastic representation of her professional trajectory.  In the bottom right, you will see that when Christina started out in her career she followed a beautifully straight path. Even though she changed companies, working first in a large, fast-moving consumer goods company, then moving into consulting, a design agency, and finally into the world of telecoms, she felt like she had a positive career.

And then you see Christina's first peak - at the top of her career - she then faced her first redundancy. The redundancy plummeted her into a trough; she felt extremely off-course even though she was able to secure a new job within less than a year. After this event, her graph rises again, before she encounters her second redundancy in just 2 years! Whilst Christina is not unique (as the 2000 Dot-Com Bust, as it is known, hit multitudes of people worldwide), at this point, Christina felt that she had completely lost herself. Even though she managed to get into some consulting roles working as a telecoms analyst, thanks to a great mentor and colleague of hers (more of that later), she was very unsure where she was going professionally; she was very unhappy.

After these two milestones, you'll see a fluctuating movement in the graph; as anyone who is a fellow entrepreneur will know, entrepreneurship is marred with highs and lows! So, whilst the launch of Christina's retail outlet in Mayfair was exciting, it was stressful. While she was doing what she loved, combining creativity and making positive change for others, financially she was in dire straits (the graph dropping until the point of the business loss). This took its toll on Christina; she felt at the lowest of the low. She slowly worked out how to reinvent herself and rise back up again.

Christina had to Reboot, Rebuild, Reconquer™. She came up with a selection of strategies to get her through the tough times - strategies that we will share with you. Christina launched Aquitude, her consultancy firm, through which she was able to re-mould and Rebuild her career in various sectors. Whilst she was professionally recovering, the 2008 financial crisis hit, leading to a significant trough in her career.

After this crisis, Christina's career followed a steady trajectory and a generally positive trend. There was a slight plateau for a few couple of years where she was doing some consulting work in an industry of which she was not particularly fond. However, those projects helped propel her into an area of digital marketing and customer experience where she was able to do a lot of work internationally. This experience led to a great few years of traveling the world, teaching an abundance of courses and doing consulting work around e-commerce, digital marketing, social media and customer experience. Then Covid-19 hits.

IDENTIFYING LEARNINGS THROUGH YOUR LIFE MILESTONE GRAPH

As demonstrated, the Life Milestone Graph helps diagrammatically pull together your key milestones. Take a sheet of paper and draw your own graph, following the instructions above. Take a good look at your peaks and troughs. Now, carefully think back:

- What did you learn during those milestones?

- What new skills did you develop at each point?

- Think about both the soft and hard skills you may have developed. To help you distinguish them, hard skills are related to specific technical knowledge and training (e.g. engineering, program management) while soft skills are personality traits such as leadership, communication or time management. Both types of skills are necessary to successfully perform and advance in most jobs.

Some of the hard and soft skills Christina learnt as part of her first entrepreneurial venture are listed below. When she launched her retail business she developed:

- Sales skills and crisis management: she had to build a whole sales strategy for the retail outlet and learned financial crisis management (boot-strapping the business, paying it all from her own savings and a bank loan).

- Leadership skills: she was able to take her team of 5 staff through a storm, inspiring them when things were tough. When she finally did lose the business, she had to keep them positive about their future prospects, offering them as much personal support as possible.

- Resilience skills: Christina had to learn to pick herself up again! When she had to declare the business voluntarily insolvent, she had to pull her socks up and get back out there and grow, Rebuild herself and Reconquer.

In terms of hard skills, Christina learnt:

- Business management (Christina calls it the most expensive MBA you could possibly have!).

- Digital marketing: Christina created a shoppable website, gaining digital and e-commerce skills. This was a novelty in 2006 and Christina's first entry into a very digital world.

THE LIFE MILESTONE GRAPH: YOUR PERSONAL RESILIENCE-BUILDER

We are big fans of the Life Milestone Graph, as it helps to set out a visual representation of your life trajectory, with all the good and the more challenging aspects laid out. Being able to take stock of all your learnings helps you build an appreciation of what you have achieved in the good times, but also helps you embrace the power of your internal resilience. Yes, losing a business may have at first seemed like a failure, but being able to demonstrate to yourself that through challenge you acquire a set of new skills, as well as, knowledge, well, frankly, that is invaluable. It helps you reframe a negative into a positive. Whatever the challenge you may have endured, having the capacity to review it, reframe it and take the learnings forward is the foundation of a transformational leader.

As you progress through this book, you will discover that strategies like these are what make the difference in your future success. Which is why in the next chapter we will use this tool to discover the other elements which are foundational to your growth - aligning your strengths with your passions.

BOX 3: YOUR LIFE LESSONS

What did you learn during your life milestones?

How do you feel about your career or projects now that you have completed the Life Milestone Graph?

Do you see where the strongest points of your life, or your career lie? Which gave you the most learnings?

Remember, it is not only the good that teaches you - hardships are also a fantastic source of wisdom!

# REBOOT REBUILD RECONQUER

# CHAPTER 4
# ALIGNING STRENGTHS
# WITH PASSIONS

*'The good life consists in deriving happiness by using your signature strengths every day in the main realms of living. The meaningful life adds one more component: using these same strengths to forward knowledge, power or goodness.'* Martin Seligman

## Strengths and Passions

When living through extraordinary change, our whole world changes. Here, we must not underestimate the impact of change. It is going to rock us to the core. Our foundations are going to feel uncertain, even ready to crumble. Whether it is redundancy, a feeling of 'my-life-could-be-better' or a health-shock, when we are forced into a new reality very often our value - system also changes.

As we spend most of our life in work (paid or unpaid, or just passion projects), reviewing the drivers behind that very system is fundamental.

THE FOUNDATIONS FOR HAPPINESS

Martin Seligman is often called the father of Positive Psychology and in his 2002 book *Authentic Happiness*, he proposed the 'orientations' of being happy, including:

- Pleasure: An individual leading a life of pleasure can be seen as maximizing positive emotions, and minimizing negative emotions.

- Engagement: An individual leading a life of engagement constantly seeks out activities that allow her to be in flow. Flow, coined by Mihály Csíkszentmihályi, is a state of deep, effortless involvement. It occurs most frequently when we concentrate our undivided attention on activities that are moderately challenging to us. When you are in flow, it may seem that your sense of self vanishes and time stops.

- Meaning: An individual leading a life of meaning belongs to and serves something that is bigger than himself. These larger entities could be family, religion, community, country, or even ideas.[6]

WHY YOU NEED TO ALIGN YOUR STRENGTHS WITH YOUR PASSIONS

You may recall our first book, *Your Loss: How to Win Back Your Female Talent*, which we mentioned in the foreword and for which we undertook quantitative and qualitative research, interviewing and surveying women from around the world. We discovered that the reason why women took change into their own hands and pivoted, leaving behind their corporate track was because they were not fulfilled. In fact, over a third (36%) of our respondents said that they were not satisfied, that their heart wasn't in what they were doing anymore. It is really interesting that as we go down our career / life path, what gratifies us seems to shift. This has been something that we have

---

[6] Source:https://livingmeanings.com/martin-seligman-and-his-two-theories-of-happiness/

seen with clients and organizations all over the planet, which is why as part of our Reboot strategy, it is important to align our passions with our strengths.

YOU ARE EXCELLENT AT SOMETHING!

We go through life always being critical of ourselves. In the early days of our careers, we are told we have to work on our weaknesses. Our feedback structures are set up to destroy our confidence, managers all too often focusing on our areas for improvement. We disagree wholeheartedly with the management styles of today. Christina was once told she 'smiles too much' as part of her feedback review. We understand that there are times when we may need to adapt our style to a situation, but the feedback Christina received for example, was generic. If smiling is something that comes naturally (and Christina does a lot of it!) then a skilled manager should not attempt to change the person, but rather change the job or projects to suit the employee's strengths. Christina's smile is an indication of her excellent people skills, so perhaps a role in client or account management, sales prospecting or training could have been options that a skilled manager would look into. Christina would have excelled in all of them.

In the same way Christina smiles a lot (and adds value!), you too do something you are good at which has relevance to your employer or organisation. This is part of the challenging realities of today's work environment: we're fed a diet of not what we are good at but what we need to work on. Managers are often saying 'well, you need to work on A, B, C, D' rather than saying, 'you know what? You're so good at this, build on it'. This is one of the mindset shifts that we have to work through in this book, starting right now.

In order to discover your strengths, we invite you to take 30 seconds to write down what you are good at – both at work and in your down-time. Try and remember when others have told you that you are good at something. Don't take long, you probably already know deep down what you are good at, you just need to dig it out. This impulsive response opens the window on your innate strengths. It could be doing research, prospecting, building relationships with others, devising new products and much, much more. Write it all down! If you need a bit more of a nudge, the achievements on your Life Milestone Graph from Chapter 3 will also help you.

Now that you have written down the things that you are good, if not excellent, at, we invite you to remind yourself of those moments where you shone. If they are not in your Life Milestone Graph, add them! Think all the way back to your school days and the subjects and extra-curricular activities you may have excelled in.

*'In strength there is power; in passion there is longevity.'*
Christina Ioannidis

When we utilise our strengths, we feel an innate power. However, if we are not passionate about it, then we will not go far. It is the worst thing in the world to work on something that we may be great at but have no passion for and vice versa. In order to go far, your strengths and your passions have to be aligned: This allows you to be authentic to who you are and it will energise rather than drain you.

If you had a magic wand, what would you be doing right now? What would you be working on? It could be anything: setting up a charity, climbing Mount Everest - any answers are relevant. Go crazy because we want you to think big!

Very often, Christina is told by clients that they have no passion. She uses the following five questions to help uncover their potential hidden gems of excitement. With this aim, she has devised the Passion Equation, an exercise repeated below which helps her delegates and clients discover what makes their heart sing.

## THE PASSION EQUATION

Now that you have jogged your memory by going over your career, see if you can identify any more stand-out passions for yourself. Go back to your sheet and re-read the questions. Relate these now back to your strengths.

---

### BOX 4: RETURNING TO THE PASSION QUESTIONS

1. When do you feel free? When are you relaxed and not worried about anything? You can write anything but please be specific. e.g. is it when you are exercising, painting or sailing?

2. What did you used to enjoy or love doing as a child? e.g. Christina loving acting as a child aligns with her strength in performing and serves her in what she does today.

3. What gets you out of bed in the morning? What are the things that you enjoy doing so much that you can't wait to jump out at the world? What are the things that you're constantly thinking of, dreaming of, striving for? We're hoping there's at least one thing that you'll be able to identify.

4. When does time run away with you? What are you doing when you feel so happy and relaxed that you forget that time even exists? What could you do for hours on end? It might be painting, reading, writing, talking to friends or presenting an idea.

5. What one thing would you change in the world?

---

*'Frustration is a great source of inspiration',* Dame Anita Roddick

The quote above is very relevant for anyone who feels they have no passion. Dame Anita Roddick, launched the Body Shop when she wasn't able to find cruelty-free cosmetics.  Her motivation was led by the resolution of a problem, which is why the last question is: 'What one thing would you change in the world?' For example, are you someone who might be interested in stopping child trafficking, or breast cancer or climate change? How would you contribute to that change? There may be one charity or one cause that you would support. Be as specific as you can.

Spend some time answering these questions and take a good look at your answers. From these answers, think about the areas that you would like to focus on more in your day-to-day. What are the things that you have forgotten you enjoyed so much?

Remember the lady who discovered that time ran away with her when she was working with plants? She realised the huge sense of satisfaction she found from doing gardening work and letting her plants flourish. Horticulture was something latent in her life and an opportunity for her future career transition. Do not feel or discard anything that you may have written down because it could be a nugget or an indicator of what you may be interested in pursuing more of in the future.

In the next exercise we will align your passions and your strengths. The following table consists of four columns: in the first column, log your passions or the things that frustrate you; in the second, note your strengths; in the third, think about how your current or future aspirations leverages those strengths, and in the final column write what you would need to do in order for that role to utilize those strengths.

# Aligning your Passions & Strengths

## Passions

- List out your top three passions
- List out things that frustrate you

## Your Strengths

- What are your key strengths?

## Leveraging Your Strengths

- How does your current role/future ambition leverage your strengths?

## Utilising Your Strengths

- What would you need to do or what would need to happen for your role or future ambition to utilise strengths?

We will break this down for you with an example from Christina. She did this exercise to come up with her current business which she has been running since 2007.

- In column one, she wrote that her passion was all about performing, storytelling and inspiring others. She enjoys multi-sensory learning experiences but hates lecture-type training.

- In column two, she wrote that her strengths were creativity, flexibility, performance, persistence, resilience and cultural adaptability.

- In column three, she realised that she could utilise her performance and creativity skills in her alternative, multi-sensory training business. She would realise an individual or companies' talent by incorporating creativity into soft and hard skills development.

- In column four, she saw that in order for her to fulfill this ambition and utilize her strengths, she would have to build her credibility by creating a portfolio of training programs and becoming known as a trainer worldwide. She would need to construct a niche which she could be recognized as contributing towards.

Writing her first book with Nicola was one way of helping her to create that niche around the subject of Diversity and Inclusion. She also decided she would focus on multinational corporations and build a reputation in international training.

Make sure you spend the time filling out each column. We're hoping you can fill out all of them but if you can't, feel free to take a step back, think about it and then try again. We're confident that you will be able to do it because if Christina can do it, so can you! Open up that pandora's box of strengths and passions!

In the box below is a completed example of this exercise from one of Christina's boot camp graduates. What's so good about this example is that you can clearly see the process by which you can aspire to be in roles that fulfil and utilise your strengths.

# Aligning your Passions & Strengths

## Passions

Passion for helping companies deliver holistic strategies

I'd love to be the main external spokesperson overseeing the development and commercial strategies of a company – CHIEF COMMERCIAL OFFICER and/or Commercial Director, who more specifically helps their company maintain a consistent trajectory of growth, while avoiding obstacles that arise from a constantly shifting market.

Public Speaking (story telling)

## Your Strengths

Connecting with people

Solving Problems

Analysing Data

Working on new ideas

## Leveraging Your Strengths

Working with teams and analysing data to develop strategic plans to steer the company sales and marketing

Promote and expand the company's commercial activity that will generate revenues and lead to sustainable growth

Pricing, Comp+ Ben, Sales Budget, Marketing Budget

Creative ways to generate additional sources of income

## Utilising Your Strengths

To be a Chief Commercial Officer I need to first become a Commercial Director

To become a Commercial Director I need to … Brush up my financial acumen and Strategic Business Management

In the First Column, she wrote that her goal in life was to become a Chief Commercial Officer. She was someone who was passionate about helping companies by offering them holistic experiences. Her goal associated with this passion was to be a holistic internal strategist and external spokesperson and oversee the development of the commercial strategies of a company. She also understood that in order to achieve this role and help companies maintain a consistent trajectory for growth, she would have to build strategies to avoid failing in a shifting market. She also had a passion for public speaking, with a very strong story-telling angle.

In the second column, she wrote that her strengths were connecting with people, solving problems, analysing data and working on new ideas.

In the third column, she wrote working with teams and analysing data to develop strategic plans and steer the company in sales and marketing. By working through this exercise, she realised that a sensible stepping stone would be a Commercial Director role.  Using these traits she had outlined she'd be able to achieve her goal of having the traits needed as a Chief Commercial Officer and in her stepping stone of potentially being a Commercial Director, she would need to promote and expand the company's commercial activity to generating revenues that would lead to sustainable growth. This would involve looking at pricing, compensation benefits, sales budgets, marketing budgets etc. and identifying creative ways to create additional sources of income and putting these into action. If she could successfully demonstrate these skills and execute them she would be in a position to progress into her desired role.

In the last column, she realised that she would need to achieve the stepping stone of working as a commercial director before achieving her final ambition of becoming a Chief Commercial Officer. She would achieve that intermediary stepping stone by using the traits she had outlined.

In moments of change, self-reflection and introspection will help you find your path; aligning your strengths and passions helps build the path.

We cannot stress enough the power of this chapter. We encourage you to take advantage of this point of inflection in your life to aim for the pursuit of your innate happiness. Aligning your strengths and passions enables you to derive pleasure and engagement on a new path which awaits you!

---

**BOX 5: ALIGNING STRENGTHS AND PASSIONS**

Write down what you are excellent at doing - use your Life Achievements Graph for inspiration.

Answer the 5 questions in the Passion Equation

Complete the Aligning Passions and Strengths table

When you have completed the 3 exercises above…:

What did you discover?

Are there any surprises for you in your answers?

Can you find ways to connect your strengths with passions in ways you may not have considered before?

Talk through this table with someone you respect in your life. What do they think about how you can align your strengths and passions?

---

# REBOOT REBUILD RECONQUER

# CHAPTER 5
# PERSONAL CONTRIBUTIONS:
# THE CATALYST TO CONFIDENCE BUILDING

## Money talks!

When we go through personal transformation, our confidence is rocked. When we have to pivot our lives or careers, the one thing we need the most is confidence. So, in this section we will focus on articulating your personal contributions.

We appreciate that material items and income levels should not dictate how worthy we feel about ourselves, however we are firm believers that when we consciously identify the monetary value we have brought to our organisations, jobs, or projects, our confidence is boosted. Why? Money is a proxy we can accept to provide an indication of achievement. As money is tangible, it is easy for us to build a mental picture of something we have brought to our employers or projects. We have seen this with our multitude of clients and workshop delegates- we see the bright spark that shines in their eyes when they can aptly communicate how much they have brought to their institution. The change in confidence is visible!

WHY MONEY TALKS

No one in business school or business teaches us this critical element. When it comes to rebooting your life or career, it is essential to be able to quantify your achievements. Why? Money does talk!

Let's make one thing clear: we are not obsessed with making money at any cost. We both have strong ethics and have deliberately made life choices (Nicola in caring for her family, and Christina in caring for her father) that have enabled us to sustain balance and better quality relationships in our personal lives, rather than a big shiny pay cheque. However, what gets measured gets done and without a fundamental understanding of finances, you are on a slippery slope to nowhere. You must be able to quantify these things in order to succeed in any walk of life. It is a matter of personal integrity.

When the chips were down in the property development for The Orange Tree Hub, Nicola was able to properly quantify the financial situation and keep her business partners on board. Her being in control of the numbers gave them confidence to stick around even when the project was sucking money down the drain (that's a story for another day - there was a literal drain problem!). Don't be scared; it's not as hard as people think.

Let us explain. As you progressed through your career, you worked on projects or activities that somehow contributed to your business. Everything we do has an impact. More often than not, this impact is linked to either making money or saving money for a business. In entrepreneur land this can be the difference between bankruptcy and profitability.

SO, HOW DO YOU CALCULATE YOUR PERSONAL CONTRIBUTION?

How does this work? It is quite simple. In business, there are two essential ways a business operates: by generating revenue (sales) and by lowering its costs (savings). Every department in the business does either one or the other, as summarized by the image opposite.

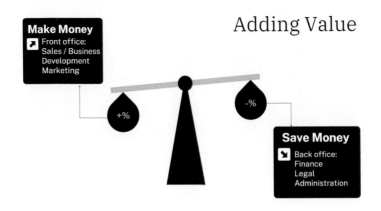

If you are in a department such as sales or marketing, you are responsible for bringing in cash - you are generating money for the business. In the back-office, you may not always be customer-facing, but much of the time you are busy creating efficiencies, helping the business save money. These departments are fundamental to running the business efficiently and preventing money going out faster than it comes in. If you are an entrepreneur you do all of the above!

As you go through your career it is essential that you can prove to a future employer (or business partner if you are looking to go into entrepreneurship) that you are an asset to the business. An asset is something that helps a business make money. If you are able to quantify your contributions, you not only demonstrate that you understand the fundamental premises of business, but you also prove that you can do the same for them. In this way, you will stand out from the other potential 'competitors' for the role.

Additionally, being able to talk in the language of business (whether we like it or not) makes you more appealing when you are transitioning or when you are transferring to a different industry or company.

CALCULATING YOUR OWN PERSONAL CONTRIBUTION

To calculate how much you may have made or saved a business, let's imagine you are working in a sales department which traditionally generated sales of 50 USD per customer before you arrived. The number of customers was 1,000. Now, with your involvement, you increased sales per customer to 55 USD and you increased the number of customers to 1,500. You increased sales from 50 x 1,000 = 50,000 USD to 55 x 1,500 USD = 82,500. Therefore, you were able to increase the revenue the business generated by 60% ((50,000/82,500)x100).

Let's look at it from the other side. Let's imagine you work in a finance department. One of the biggest challenges that businesses have is managing the timeframe in which customers pay them. If you work in a large organization and you have multiple customers, it is likely that the typical payment terms are about 60 days or two months. In order to make up for the shortfall while waiting for the money to arrive, businesses borrow from the bank. As an example, let's just say that through your work you sped up the payment timeframe of customers, so instead of them paying in 60 days, you somehow manage to get them to pay in 30 days. So, you're essentially saving the business 30 days of bank interest.

Now, let's imagine your business borrows at an interest rate of 6% per year for the purposes of working capital. Alternative to receiving the money today is to borrow that cash from the bank (or if it's a development loan, 15%!).

**$1000 today vs $1000 in 30 days which means you borrow for 30 days at 6% = $1000x0.06/12=$5**

You saved $5 per customer by tightening up the payment terms.  This works in the reverse if you negotiate a longer time to pay people you owe money to. Big supermarkets are masters at this and they often cause problems for their suppliers (farmers and such like) with their extremely long payment terms.

If this were an easy exercise, then everyone would do it. But the reality is, no one teaches us how to do this. However, we believe this is one of the most important skills to own when you are looking to pivot. Whilst you may not be an expert in a particular industry or sector, the fact that you can talk numbers to a potential employer or even, an investor, makes you a more appealing asset.

So, this is where we will invite you to spend some time looking at your personal contributions - have you made money or have you saved money? The steps to work this out are:

1.  Look at your Life Milestone Graph, and look at different roles you may have had.

2.  Identify if you were in the front office (a revenue contributor) or back office (you helped save the business money).

3.  For each role, you need to consider how much you may have made or saved a business, as per above.

We would encourage you to start by making this calculation for one of your achievements. Hopefully once you have done it for one, you can then do it for others. Pick two or three and get to quantifying the full amount of time, savings or revenue that you might have saved or generated for your business or project.

## A word about Not-for-Profits / Charities

We would like to mention working for not-for-profit businesses or charities, which some people mistakenly assume don't generate revenue. They have to fundraise, and even though you might not consider it revenue, fundraising is still an income-generating activity. By the same token, charities have to manage their costs in exactly the same way as a normal business; they have to finely balance covering their operational costs and raising enough funds so as to do so. What charities don't do is save the profit and give it to the shareholders in the same way that profit making companies do.

VALUE YOUR WORTH, ALWAYS

We hope that you do not think we are being hard-nosed, but by taking the time to consider your contribution to your previous, or future businesses/projects, you are also embracing the importance of valuing your worth. We are not educated nor encouraged, for that matter, to keep tabs of what we bring to the table for our employers unless you are in a sales-role. We believe that this is completely wrong. By being able to quantify our contribution we also empower ourselves with confidence, confidence that our influence, our input, can fuel the bottom line of our business.

This confidence, we hope, will lay the foundation for attaining, or even creating, the future roles and businesses you desire. In the post-Covid19 world, we need to be able to create personal strategies that can give us a leg up and stand out in a very competitive world. We also need to be able to have the internal strength to flex our mental muscles and build resilience within us. Knowing our worth is one of these strategies, as far as we are concerned.

We also encourage you to do this on an ongoing basis and not just when you may be looking to pivot. By reviewing your achievements (keep the Life Milestone Graph with you as a 'live' document) and at each step quantifying your contributions, you will be able to confidently convey what you offer to your project/business at the drop of a hat. We have found that clients who do this as part of the personal rebooting build great internal strength and can thrive even in the hardest of times.

Now that you have completed your rear-view mirror exercise, in the next chapter we will move into the Rebuilding Phase where we will start taking all of these inputs to look at the new, exciting future which may lie ahead of you.

---

**BOX 6: YOUR CONTRIBUTIONS**

Review your Life Milestone Graph, and look at different roles you may have had or projects you may have been involved with

Identify if you were in the front office (a revenue contributor) or back office (you helped save the business money)

For each role, figure out how much you may have made or saved a business?

Look at the figures generated.

How do you feel about those numbers? Are you surprised by the outcome?

How do you feel about knowing how much you have brought to your business or project?

---

# REBOOT REBUILD RECONQUER

## CHAPTER 6
## REBUILDING:
## BUSINESS AS UNUSUAL

*'Within the next two years, 72 percent of people working today will be in different jobs in the same or different companies and have different responsibilities requiring different talents and skills to achieve different results. And those people who fail to respond to the challenges of change will be most affected by it.'*
Brian Tracy[7]

## Developing Your Vision

We have gone through lots of exercises, thinking and processing the journey of your career, your life, and how we have gotten to where we are. Taking the time to process where we have come from gives us the grounding we need for any future transformations. We have also learned how to articulate our value in financial terms, a fundamental element which enables us to build our confidence.

We are now at a point where we will revisit our strengths and our passions. One of the most important things we

---

[7] Source: Reinvention: How to Make the Rest of Your Life the Best of Your Life, page 3 Tracy, Brian

have discovered by working with clients and companies around the world is that if we don't align strengths and passions, we find that people feel like they're leading a life that is not worth their commitment. In our previous research, we found that the number one reason why women were leaving corporations is because they were not fulfilled. Women are not the only ones doing so. The Great Resignation which we have already mentioned is a clear example where the pandemic has impacted the internal value of work, irrespective of gender, age or ethnicity.

As we progress through any journey of transformation, we will inherently face moments of insecurity. We will also doubt ourselves and our abilities (more on that below), so as a leader driving change, it is imperative you hone in on what really makes you tick. In doing so, you will be refreshed, even rejuvenated, by the knowledge that you are utilising your strengths and passions going forward.

It is therefore very important for us to spend a long time looking into this topic. Let's return to the four columned table from Chapter 4. The first is your passions and frustrations - Dame Anita Roddick said, *'frustration is a great source of inspiration'*. The second, strengths. The penultimate column how our current work or our future ambitions leverage these strengths. The last column is what we need to happen in order for our role or future ambition to fully utilise our strengths.

BUSINESS AS UNUSUAL: REBOOTING FOR THE FUTURE

Dame Anita Roddick wrote the book *Business as Unusual;* she titled it this because she went down a route that was not expected of her when she created her business The Body Shop.

# REBOOT REBUILD RECONQUER

Eleanor Mills, award winning, top-flight Editor in British national newspapers for over two decades speaks of her personal identity crisis which hit her when she went through an unexpected redundancy after 25 years at a newspaper:

*'I took off that cloak and laid it down. I thought it was important to do that. Underneath I felt like the creature in Alien, or something, like this kind of weird thing underneath Darth Vader, that nobody has actually seen. Nobody has actually seen you without your cloak, without your armour for a really long time, in fact you haven't really seen yourself.'*

When you remove your metaphorical cloak of your past roles, you are hit with a vulnerable moment of insecurity on... who is the real you?

In order to overcome that potential identity crisis we will help you look at unexpected roots that are going to create the future you. By the end of the chapter, you will be ready to create your Transformation Vision Board - a powerful visualisation technique.

We are big fans of a technique that leadership guru Brian Tracy advocates - working with your '5-year fantasy'. Think of your five-year fantasy, take a step back and project yourself into the future. Don't be limited by where you are now.

---

**BOX 7: DEVELOP YOUR 5 YEAR FANTASY PICTURE**

To build that 5 year fantasy, consider:

> What is your desire?
>
> Where do you want to be?
>
> What will you be doing in your life, in your career?
>
> What about your hobbies and extracurricular activities?

---

Use your answers to build a mental picture, then write down what you saw. It has been proven by research that those who have a vision are more likely to achieve their aspirations if they have visualised them.

Christina did this exercise when she went through her serious career transformation (post double-redundancy and business failure). She wrote that she will be training globally (using the word 'will' will help to actualise fantasies), addressing international audiences, delivering five-day courses and immersing herself in different cultures. Guess what? This became her reality!

Next, we want you to think about what you DON'T want from your career or future aspirations. What we don't want to happen to us can help us realise what we do want. Christina didn't want a boss that didn't recognise her strengths and talents. So, she created her own company and role as a consultant and external trainer. Now, she doesn't have a formal boss that she has to depend on, her clients are the ones who give her feedback.

List those things you categorically don't want in your life or your career. Think about your personal relationships with people, the work itself and auxiliary things such as travel. Consider those things that impact the quality of your work and life. Write them down. Once more, visualise the scenarios in which these could happen and the lack of fulfilment they could lead to.

Compare the two lists and realise the positives of what you do want against what you do not want. By assimilating what you have written, you are starting to build a clear picture of what your future will look like.

TIME AND FOCUS: ESSENTIALS TO ACHIEVING YOUR 5-YEAR FANTASY

We will now focus on building the strategies to achieve your desired future. This is often the point where people start feeling uncomfortable in their personal or career transformation. A little internal voice makes itself known, saying "I'm not sure if this is what I want", "Would it be too aggressive?", "Do I deserve this?". We advise that you move into this discomfort zone, it is a sign of the transformation from the old you to the new you. Remember this process is called Reboot, Rebuild, Reconquer™ for a reason. But stay away from limiting beliefs of negatives - what you need to do is focus.

We are now on the cusp of the rebuilding phase. Right now, you are setting the foundations for the Rebuild and managing your expectations. It's going to take you between one and five years to get to where you want to be; it's not going to be a quick fix. You might say you can't wait five years, that it's too long. True, it does sound like a long time, but remember, while we might not achieve our fantasy until five years from now, we will achieve constant forward momentum. Christina launched her business in training and consulting in 2007, but it wasn't until 2013-14 that her globe-trotting training and speaking really took off. It took her persistence to build the business but she remained on a progressive trajectory.

## THE LAW OF ATTRACTION

As individuals, we make energy, and whatever energy we emit is also the type of energy that we are going to get back. This is the basis of the Law of Attraction. Brian Tracy writes in his book Reinvention: How to Make the Rest of Your Life the Best of Your Life:

*'The Law of Attraction says that you are a "living magnet" and that you invariably attract into your life the people, ideas, opportunities, and circumstances in harmony with your dominant thoughts. When you think positive, optimistic, loving, and successful thoughts, you create a force field of magnetism that attracts, like iron filings to a magnet, the very things you are thinking about. This law explains why it is that you don't have to be concerned where your good is going to come from. If you can keep your mind clearly focused on what you want, and refrain from thinking about what you don't want, you will attract everything you need to achieve your goals, exactly when you are ready. Change your thinking and you change your life. One of the great dangers of experiences, a sudden verse or unexpected transition in your life, is you can very easily interpret the experience in a negative way. When you do this, quite innocently, you set up a force field of negative energy that attracts even more negative experiences into your life. This is the meaning of the saying when it rains, it pours.'* [8]

You can create a positive force field by focusing on a five-year fantasy that you will achieve. It is really more practical than you might imagine: You will already be behaving in the way that 'new future' you will behave. Your actions

---

[8] Source: Reinvention: How to Make the Rest of Your Life the Best of Your Life. page 41. Tracy. Brian

will be aligned with what you want and the people around you will respond accordingly.

The capacity to succeed is directly related to your positive energy and momentum. This has been proven by research. In 1953, a study was conducted looking at 300 graduates of top universities in the US, exploring how many of them had a clear vision of where they wanted to be in the future. The majority did not have a vision upon graduation of what they wanted to do. Only 3% of them had actually written down what they hoped to achieve or where they wanted to be. Twenty years later, this research was reviewed: the 3% who had written down their visions had achieved them as well as having made more money than the other 97% combined.[9]

The power of our minds and visualisations are an extraordinary tool for success. CEOs do it. People in high-performance industries do it. Athletes do it. Even patients do it. If you want to get better, visualise yourself getting better; envision yourself using whatever limb that may have been injured. Christina herself had an extremely bad accident in 2009 and lost the use of her right (and dominant) hand for about nine months. She was in physiotherapy for six months. What she realised was that when she visualised moving her hand, it helped her to reprogram her mind. If we know what we want, our mind can help us get there.

---

9 Source: Reinvention: How to Make the Rest of Your Life the Best of Your Life. Page 54. Tracy. Brian

THE TRANSFORMATION VISION BOARD

To help you practice this technique and move your personal transformation forward, we're going to create a vision board. Take a mental inventory of what you want your life, your project, your career to look like and write your ideas down. Hand write your goals, don't type them. Now, take a piece of paper and think of mental images, quotes or anything which reflects your future aspirations, goals and desires. Take these back to your five-year fantasy and bring it to life. Get online, find your scrapbooks or Pinterest boards and find advice, quotes, photos, scenes, images of places you want to go, reminders of events - anything that will inspire you and get them onto your vision board! The most important thing is that you physically go through this process.

When it is done, share it with others, show them your intentions and talk them through your goals. The more we talk and collaborate on what we want, the more we manifest that vision and opportunities to achieve our desires arise.

As an example, we will glance at a career vision board done by the aspiring Chief Commercial Officer in Chapter 4.  Of course, no two aspiration boards are the same, just as no two fingerprints are the same, but you may take some inspiration from the things this individual envisioned for herself. Her images included a female leader, the motto 'push yourself because no one else is going to do it for you', a woman shown caring for two people, money (after all, she wants compensation for her performance), a first-class travel ticket, being affirmed by others and finally, a sunset, to remind herself to relax and enjoy the moment. She found that the more she visualised her goal, the more she became confident of her self-worth.

As you progress through your journey of transformation, your Transformation Vision Board is a powerful visualization technique which helps to cement, solidify and crystallise your long-term goals. It is the crutch which you can turn to when you are facing any moments of self-doubt (which, believe us, will appear). In those moments, the ability to dig deep into feelings of inspiration will propel you forward, and this is exactly what the Transformation Vision Board does!

## BOX 8: YOUR OWN TRANSFORMATION VISION BOARD

Invest the time in finding the assets you will include. When you have completed it answer these questions.

1. How far does your Transformation Vision Board help you to visualize your five year fantasy?

2. Is there anything that is on your Transformation Vision Board which surprises you?

3. Are there any themes which you can identify and are standing out for you?

4. Is there anything that may be missing from your board that could further your motivation? If so, add it!

# REBOOT REBUILD RECONQUER

# CHAPTER 7
# PERSONAL REBUILDING: UNDERSTANDING PERSONAL BRANDING

*'Becoming the best version of yourself requires you to continuously edit your beliefs, and to upgrade and expand your identity'.* James Clear[10]

BUILDING BRANDYOU 2.0!

As we move forward in our journey of transformation, there is one more fundamental element we need to figure out. Until now we have spent some time thinking about our practical strengths and passions, as well as developing visions and aspirations for what we want and don't want from our career or life. In the last chapter, we concluded by building a *Transformation Vision Board* - a manifestation of what we want from our five-year fantasy.

You may wonder, what is the next step? We need to work on demonstrating the habits that will get us to move forward to our future vision. Here we draw on the powerful work of James Clear, author of Atomic Habits, who states that:

*'Your behaviors are usually a reflection of your identity. What you do is an indication of the type of person you believe that you are — either*

---

[10] *Source: Atomic Habits, James Clear, Page 36*

*consciously or non-consciously. Research has shown that once a person believes in a particular aspect of their identity, they are more likely to act in alignment with that belief. Doing the right thing is easy. After all, when your behavior and your identity are fully aligned, you are no longer pursuing behavior change. You are simply acting like the type of person you already believe yourself to be.'[11]*

This is the chapter where we work to align ourselves with the vision we aim to embody. If we aim to transform from a couch-potato to a svelte gym aficionado, we can only do so when we can associate ourselves with BEING that gym-goer. It will not be enough to just focus on trying to 'remember' to go to the gym; only when we visualise ourselves and talk to ourselves as the 'healthy gym-nut' will we be able to make our transformation happen. Why? Because in doing so we are rewiring our brains to build the mental image that we CAN be the person we aim to be. Which is where we come to focusing on your BrandYou 2.0.

WHY DO YOU EVEN NEED BRAND*YOU 2.0?*

Now, it does not matter whether you are a professional, entrepreneur or CEO of the home, we believe that one of the most important skills we all have to master in the fluid world in which we live is the power of building your personal brand as you transform into the future you.

Branding is absolutely everywhere, and this includes at the individual level. Yes, we all have a personal brand; it is the reputation of who we are and what we stand for. We are therefore going to get to know your current brand story and brand audit.

---

[11] *Source: Atomic Habits, page 34*

Let's do a quick exercise. Take a glance at this list of brands and consider the first thing that comes into your head:

- McDonalds

- Nike

- Google

- Apple

- Samsung

- Amazon

- Twitter

- Instagram

Is it a picture, a logo or an image perhaps that crops up?

What we can learn from this exercise is that a brand is essentially an association. It conjures up a sensory picture. All of the above are such strong brands because they form part of your day to day interactions. They create loyalty.

A brand is the unique, identifiable essence of a business, product or service. The process of branding, meanwhile, is the optimization of the associations, feelings and impressions that your intended target audience experiences as a result of interacting with your brand.

As the owner of BrandYou 2.0, you have to consider yourself a business owner. Why? Branding is an asset - McDonald's and Nike are valued in the millions of dollars, purely because of the powerful associations and emotions they convey to their customers and stakeholders.

By the same token, your personal brand is a widely

recognized and largely uniform preconception of you as an individual; it is a set of impressions that other people hold about you. It is based on your experiences, expertise, competencies, actions and achievements within a community, an industry or marketplace at large.

REVIEWING YOUR CURRENT BRAND

Let's do a quick review of your current brand. Think about yourself. When others think about you, what associations do you inspire in their mind? In fact, are you memorable in any way? How strong is your brand? These are hard questions to answer about yourself, as we don't think of ourselves as a brand. This is where we encourage you to ask your friends and colleagues. Ask these questions, in confidence, and listen to the responses.

Of course, your friends and family will always try to be positive and paint you with a favourable brush. So, let's try another exercise. Google yourself and see what happens. How do you appear? What links come up? What comes up first? What makes you stand out? For example, is it your LinkedIn profile, an article, or your current employer's website which comes up top? Or is it your Facebook page or twitter account?

Based on how you appear, think about who knows you and for what? What are other people who are landing on the Google results page associating you with? What do you think are the first things that come into their mind about you? Take a step back here and be cut-throat with your answers. Self-criticism can be beneficial.

Now, here we have to focus on a point which often brings up controversy. Lots of people we have worked with, trained, and coached feel uncomfortable with these exercises. They think that their 'work' will do the talking for them, but this is a very common misconception. There are simply too many people and too much competition out there for you to think like this. No one is going to give you work, responsibility, or support you just because of how 'good' you think you are. They will give you what you desire only if they can see the power of your conviction based on your expertise, reputation and achievements. In other words, your brand. What we need to do as leaders is to define our brand shape and build it as we progress through our journey of transformation.

IDENTIFYING YOUR BRAND STORY TO-DATE

So now, let's begin to think about what *you* have to say about yourself. Keep in mind the following definition of personal branding as, 'the conscious and intentional effort to create and influence public perception of an individual by positioning them as an authority in their industry, someone who differentiates themself from the competition to ultimately advance their career, increase their circle of influence and have a larger impact.'[12]

With your experience and life to-date you have invariably created a brand. In Chapter 3, you were asked to think about your Personal Achievements and were tasked with creating a Life Achievements Graph. Going forward, these achievements will tell a key part of your brand story. Review your graph, career/life milestones, experiences, learnings, skills, strengths and passions. Which ones would you carry forward into the future you? What are the small wins that you have experienced in the past which show you that you have the ability to overcome whatever challenge is thrown your way? Think about each one of these areas as the legs of a stool - if your future brand is the top of the stool, which of these would imbalance the stool if it were missing? As you start to building your BrandYou 2.0, we encourage you to take the

---

[12] Source: https://personalbrand.com/definition

most important elements from your past into your future. Don't cut corners here, the more time you spend thinking about it, the stronger your brand will be. Feel free to use some creative license.

INVEST IN BUILDING BRANDYOU 2.0

In this chapter we have taken a 'rearview mirror' approach to your personal brand. We have covered why, in this time of tumultuous change, it is important to build your inner strength and resiliency by tapping into the elements of your past that support the new you. Whilst in the next chapter we will build on that future brand, do invest the time to introspect deeply. Only when we have filled our internal tanks with the personal recognition of what we have achieved and what that means for our credibility, knowledge and reputation, can we build on a brave new version of ourselves which reflects... our rebooted self!

---

BOX 9: FILTERING YOUR LIFE ACHIEVEMENTS GRAPH

Which are the milestones, experiences, learnings, skills, strengths and passions that you would carry forward into the future you?

Think about each one of these areas as the legs of a stool - if your future brand is the top of the stool, which of these would imbalance the stool if it were missing?

---

# CHAPTER 8
# BUILDING YOUR
# BRANDYOU 2.0 STORY

*'Develop high personal standards and then live by them. Demand more from yourself—no exceptions. Operate from a larger, more inclusive perspective. Strive to be more understanding and compassionate of others. Take 100% responsibility for your actions and your results. Class acts take responsibility for their actions instead of hiding, blaming others, or making excuses. Add something of value in all situations. Pursue big goals that require you to grow. Bring value to the world.'* Jack Canfield[13]

## Redressing the Gaps in Your Brand Story

Transformation is hard, and you will be a different person to the one you were in the past once you complete your journey. As mentioned in the previous chapter, allowing yourself the time to Rebuild the new BrandYou 2.0 is important. You will now be walking in a brand new mindset, a brand new approach to life, with different aspirations to those of the past.

In this chapter, we will focus on your Brand Story for the future. Why? BrandYou 2.0, the new you that you will exemplify going forward, should, ideally, complement your 5-year fantasy. We believe that, as Jack Canfield states in the quote above, this is a prime opportunity for

---

[13] *Source: Success Affirmations: 52 Weeks for Living a Passionate and Purposeful Life. Page 98. Canfield, Jack*

you to now craft your authentic brand that reflects the new you, one which brings value to the world and others!

In the time of the Great Resignation, it is important to keep in mind that what you do has to bring meaning to your life. Why? The psychologist Martin Seligman found that the people who can make an explicit connection between their work and something socially meaningful to them are more likely to find satisfaction, and are better able to adapt to the inevitable stresses and compromises that come with working in the world.

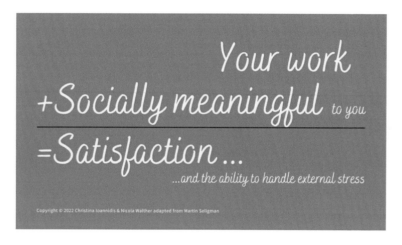

We wholeheartedly agree with this view: in this world of constant change, you need to ensure you are always on track to bring value to others, to offer something socially meaningful which fuels your feel-good tanks. This is a core element of being a transformational leader, a leader who can encourage and inspire others in some shape or form.

CRAFTING THE NEW BRANDYOU 2.0

We have defined a brand as a set of perceptions based on experiences and interactions with a product or service. We will now look at what we call the Brand DNA.

A brand is made up of four key components:

1.  Brand Essence

2.  Brand Values

3.  What you Offer

4.  Benefits you bring to others

Structurally, this works a bit like an onion, like in the diagram here:

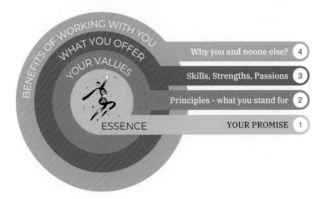

Let's take the case of Nike as an example: the essence is reaching ones human potential; the values are inspiration, challenging oneself, authenticity, purpose; the offers are acceleration, achievement, technological advancement and new materials at the forefront of the sports industry; the benefits are high performance, status, premium, innovation.

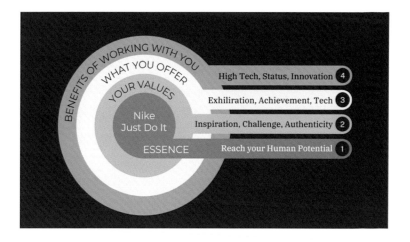

Using this model, let's work on the long-term vision for BrandYou 2.0. We are going to decipher your brand essence and everything else that supports it, step by step. Recreate the image above and fill out your answers in the appropriate circle.

ESTABLISHING YOUR BRAND DNA

## 1.Essence

To work out your essence, ask yourself the following questions:

- What do I stand for as a person?

- What do I promise to the world?

Put your answers in the center of the circle.

Whether you are a professional identifying your future career path, or someone who wants to make a lasting change in their health to become a new healthier you,

you need to build that sense of internal conviction of what you are to stand for in the future. This is what your essence reflects.

## 2. Values

Values are the behaviours which will guide your promise, your essence. If what your essence relates is bringing happiness, for example, then the values (the behaviours which you will exude) would need to support that essence.

- If people didn't know you personally, what would you want your reputation to suggest?

- What are the behaviours that you want people to associate with you?

In our 'Bringing Happiness' example, the behaviours you would want to be associated with might be inspiring others, encouraging positivity, being joyful, etc.

## 3. What you offer

Next, what do you offer to your stakeholders, your colleagues, community, your family?

This can be established by picking apart your key skills, strengths and passions, depending on your context, of course. Use the work we did in the last chapter on your brand story. Aim to pick the five elements from those categories that are most important for your personal brand; limiting your options to just 5 can help you to crystallize your key skills. For example, these could be managing change, leadership, communication skills, team work, crisis management. You might be passionate about climate change, high tech, healthcare, or artificial intelligence. What are the most important ones to get you to your five year fantasy?

Here we would like to draw your attention to an important point which often arises in our consulting and client work. When you are the CEO of your home (and yes, you are not officially 'employed', but you do have the hardest job on earth!), this exercise is relevant for you in order to define the person you want to be in the future. Just because you may not have had a traditional 'job', you have acquired skills, passions and experiences which are second to none! Think about time management (no one does this better than mothers!), multi-tasking, flexibility, problem solving and the list goes on!

## 4. Benefits of working with you

The last part for the Brand DNA, is the benefits you bring to others when they are interacting or working with you.

- What are the benefits of working with you?

- Why should anyone choose to work / be with you and no one else?

- What do you offer that no one else does?

- Why do you stand out?

This exercise establishes the core of who you are and is crucial for your five-year fantasy. The combination of answers in those circles reflect you. Your Brand DNA, like your biological DNA, is completely unique to you.

ADDRESSING THE IMPOSTOR SYNDROME

*'Each time I write a book, every time I face that yellow pad, the challenge is so great. I have written eleven books, but each time I think, 'Uh oh, they're going to find out now. I've run a game on everybody and they're going to find me out'* Maya Angelou

You have put in a lot of work to get to where you are

today. You are reading this book, and working through the strategies for becoming the new BrandYou 2.0. However, your brain will start messing with you. Instead of believing you deserve to be where you are, there are times you will sit there thinking "No, I don't deserve any of this"; even worse, you won't believe you can be the person behind that 5-year fantasy. This is the Impostor Syndrome.

## It is just your brain playing with you... So Step Back

The imposter syndrome is defined by the Oxford English Dictionary as *'the persistent inability to believe that one's success is deserved or has been legitimately achieved as a result of one's own efforts or skills'.* We would add to this definition that the imposter syndrome is a belief that you're not actually supposed to be feeling success in whatever field you are in. The reality of the imposter syndrome is that it hits everyone, even someone like Maya Angelou! If it hasn't hit you yet, it will hit you at some point. Irrespective of who you are or what you've done in the past, there will be a time when you will be overcome with self doubt. It is such a well-known and age-old phenomenon because so many people have felt it.

The Imposter Syndrome is dangerous because it creates fear and anxiety, preventing people from completing what they have started. We need to make sure that the imposter syndrome doesn't kill your momentum and drive. Luckily, picking up this book is in itself a great indication of your drive to take a new direction and transform.

When the Impostor Syndrome hits, your inner voice insists that someone made a mistake and you will soon get exposed as a loser, a failure, a fraud. It makes you feel guilty as though you have no reason to be where you are, or the person you aim to be.  When you experience the Impostor Syndrome, you assume others know more than you and that you will be found out.  The reality is usually different, however, and often You know just as much, or even more, than others know! As Rita Clifton author of *Love Your Imposter: Be Your Best Self, Flaws and All,* believes you can work with your imposter, and we totally agree with her!

Signs that you are dealing with Impostor Syndrome might be when your thoughts center around... *'It's not me....'* *'I will be found out'*. Christina faced this when she pivoted from her corporate career to her entrepreneurial journey by setting up her jewellery retailing business.  She felt pangs of uncertainty as she felt that she, too, would be found out as not being an expert or inexperienced in her field. She had to work hard on herself to address this.

Christina's success strategies? Christina made sure she became consciously aware of the conversation that was going on in her head when she would have feelings of being an impostor. She would then take a step back, look at the broader situation, understand what was triggering her uncertainty and reassure herself she had what it took to create and run her business. You can do exactly the same by following these crucial steps:

1. Recognise that you are doubting yourself when you hear that negative self-talk. And yes, it's normal to have these moments.

2. Ask yourself: 'Why am I feeling this way? What is triggering me to feel this way and to talk to myself like this?'

3. Think of why you DESERVE to be this new BrandYou 2.0. After all, you have all the strength, the conviction and the power to make this new Brand You 2.0 a reality.... Draw up a list and itemise the reasons why you DESERVE this new YOU.

4. Take a deep breath and take one action which will move you closer to that Brand You 2.0. This could

be logging in your journal all the reasons you identified in point 3, or sending an email to a new stakeholder who is going to be instrumental in you achieving your change. The point here is to just take action and not let your negative self-talk hold you back.

We can also try to visualise the Imposter Syndrome. Below, you see two circles - what you know and what you think you know. The assumption is that what you know is a very, very small subsection of what others know. The reality, however, is that what you know is probably equivalent, if not greater than, what others know. We therefore need to reframe your mindset to give you the confidence to feel and say this!

TASK: BRAND YOU 2.0 VISION BOARD

There is nothing more powerful than uniting your Transformation Vision Board with your Brand Vision Board and sparking a well-deserved sense of self-satisfaction and personal success.

So, here we invite you to use your Brand DNA (brand essence, values, offers and benefits) to create a Brand You 2.0 vision board. As you did with your Transformation Vision Board, use pictures, quotes and words. Wherever possible, these images should be of you - they might be experiences from the past or they might just be representative of you.

Take an hour to do this task and spend that time really digging deep for those words and supporting material. This will be fundamental going forward because every time the imposter syndrome hits you, you will either look at or bring up the mental image of this this BrandYou 2.0 Vision Board.

## BE THE CHANGE THAT YOU WANT TO BE

Let's return to Christina and her experience of the Imposter Syndrome. She had a turning point on her career journey when she was at a networking event in North London. Standing outside the venue, she just decided to go in as Christina Ioannidis 'the jewelry and accessories expert' (remember, until then she had been working as a corporate strategist and marketer). Although she felt like she might not be able to carry this story, she took a step back, centered herself and repeated these words loudly to herself: *'I AM Christina Ioannidis, a bespoke jewelry accessory designer and retailer'.*

What we want you to do is exactly what Christina did that day. We call this, 'be the change that you want to be'. You have to manifest change and the only way to do this is by standing tall and strong and saying it aloud.

---

**BOX 10: POWER STANCE EXERCISE**

**Exercise:** Try it now - stand up, stand tall, legs hip-distance-apart, pull your belly in and throw your shoulders back like you are on top of the world. This power stance will help you to feel your innate strength.

---

Now, say what you are. Complete the following statement: 'I am... who offers...'.

This was Christina's power stance proposition: *'I am Christina, I am a bespoke jewelry accessory designer and retailer who offers unique customized accessories for men and women so that they can express their individuality.'*

Take the time to practice this a few times; you may not get it right the first time. Whatever comes up and whatever statements you make, write them down. Hopefully, you will see that you have a renewed level of confidence and power. Holding on to this feeling will help you to break your mental barrier and change the way you talk about yourself; it is the trick to overcoming your imposter syndrome.

At the NatWest Accelerator, when working on one of her entrepreneurial ventures, Nicola found herself being asked to give a one minute pitch before every meeting. This was drilled into the participants of the course, not necessarily because they would have to stand in front of a room of people presenting their idea every day, but so that if they practiced their 'pitch' regularly under pressure, they would be more likely to roll it out in some kind of coherent order when faced with someone asking them what they do.  It has been immensely useful for Nicola in a multitude of different situations.

When working with her clients and any of the businesses she invests in, Nicola now insists that entrepreneurs learn and master this pitch. Being able to succinctly describe the key elements of any business (and if you are an individual, think of yourself as the business) is critical when engaging with stakeholders.  When your own brand rolls off your tongue you will feel in sync with what you are and what you offer and it will show.

POSITIVE AFFIRMATION TOOL BOX

What does your tool box include for those moments when you hear that little voice and change feels like too much for you to deal with? The positive affirmation tools are the following:

- your Transformation Vision Board

- your Brand You 2.0 Vision Board

These visual stimuli represent your career ambitions, your brand and those moments you have felt invincible. Together, they will get you through those moments of absolute doubt, self-diminishment and limitation. We encourage you to make sure you have these handy as you go through your transformation journey. Keep them, nurture them and as you go along, you might wish to adapt them. There's no harm in changing things as your transition happens.

Take the time to complete the exercises in this chapter. This is an important piece of the puzzle to propel you with your new and powerful, all-conquering mindset. After all, you now know you are worthy of the new YOU, so let's go conquer!

---

**BOX 11: BRAND REVIEW**

Review your Brand DNA - how does what you have written reflect your 5-year fantasy?

Are you feeling doubts? If so, work through the steps to counteract your Impostor Syndrome

How does it feel having worked through the process of overcoming your Impostor Syndrome?

What has this process allowed you to discover about yourself?

---

# CHAPTER 9
## IT TAKES A VILLAGE:
## BUILDING YOUR MENTORING MESH

*It takes a village (to raise a child)* African proverb

## Mentoring Mesh: Your Personal Board of Directors

IT TAKES A VILLAGE TO ... TRANSFORM

We believe that the proverb 'It takes a Village' is very relevant to anyone going through any sort of transformation. When you are pivoting your career, mindset or work, you will experience change which will impact those around you in a significant way. As your values shift (remember your Brand DNA), then, by implication, the way you approach your life, your projects, and those around you will also shift. Having the best support from those around you is critical, which is why we are fervent supporters of you taking proactive steps to build your support network to create a tribe of people who can guide you and support you through your journey.

Most people are used to considering the importance of a single mentor, someone who is there for a long-term, two-way relationship. In our view, in times of transformation you need your 'mentoring mesh', your very own 'personal board of directors', who represent a number of different individuals from different contexts who can act as informal guides and a sounding board.

In this chapter, we will look at how to create your mentoring mesh by identifying what you can offer those informal mentors, how to become more visible to them and how to develop a mentoring proposition in order to approach those ideal supporters. We have personally used every single one of the strategies that we're going to talk about and they are powerful tools to help us move forward. This is a critical part of the re-conquering equation.

This chapter brings together your Personal Contributions that we worked on in Chapter 5 and your Brand (Personal Credibility) from the previous two chapters with the final piece of Personal Capital: your Mentoring Mesh.

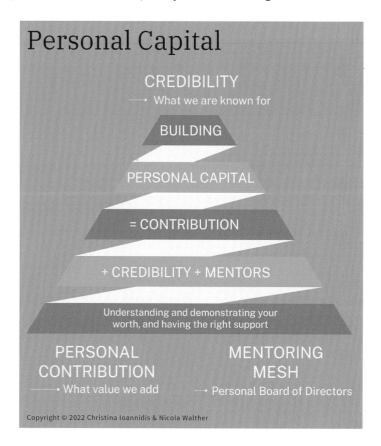

Personal Capital

CREDIBILITY
----> What we are known for

BUILDING

PERSONAL CAPITAL

= CONTRIBUTION

+ CREDIBILITY + MENTORS

Understanding and demonstrating your worth, and having the right support

PERSONAL CONTRIBUTION
----> What value we add

MENTORING MESH
----> Personal Board of Directors

Copyright © 2022 Christina Ioannidis & Nicola Walther

## Defining the Word Mentor

Let's be clear about what we mean by mentor. The word mentor comes from Homer's Odyssey, where mentor was the name of Telemachus' trusted advisor. It has been assimilated as a term meaning *'someone who imparts wisdom to and shares knowledge with a less-experienced colleague.'*[14]

In business, companies encourage employees to have someone to be supportive, take an interest in their career and assume the role of an 'official' mentor or guide. A mentor is someone who can give you advice and guide you along your professional journey. Mentoring is often associated with a formally structured relationship when one person, the mentor, has a responsibility to offer structured advice and guidance to a mentee, someone who might be looking to grow in their organization.

Sometimes, it's just someone who asks you the right questions.  Nicola had a wonderful mentor in the ex-Chairman of Schroeder's whom she met via one of her rowers.  When she was on a rowing camp, she asked Donald McDonald (of True Blue fame) if he knew someone who could mentor her in Banking, *'because the boys seemed to get plenty of help, why not her'*; what had actually been a slightly tongue in cheek question turned into a dinner the following week at a London Gentleman's Club (Nicola had to go in via the back door and she decided the venue was Donald's way of having a dig at her comment!) and introductions to three wonderful men who guided her through the next five years of her career. One of them, the aforementioned ex-Chairman, sent her faxed questions every week about the state of the market, the economy or the shareholdings and he helped her think like a Board Member long before she ever entered

---

[14] Source: Wikipedia: https://en.wikipedia.org/wiki/Mentor_(Odyssey)

the Boardroom. He also helped her with her first 'one minute pitch' or 'elevator pitch', used literally in the elevator if one was stood alongside a senior member of staff.

## MENTORING: A CRITICAL PART OF THE RECONQUERING EQUATION

While having a single mentor is a very useful relationship structure that helps to build knowledge and understanding, it is very important when we are transitioning to have a number of individuals who can function as trusted advisors. When we're pivoting from one industry or company to another, one mentor is not enough. The same goes for any context. Imagine if you are attempting to build a healthier you - you will need advisors around you who are doctors, nutritionists, personal trainers, the list goes on. The same is true if you are starting a new business - you need advice from accountants, lawyers, industry experts, financial advisors etc.

As you transform, you need to think outside of where you may be operating today. So, we encourage you to think about the individuals of influence that could help you shift into that new space you are hoping to occupy in the future. This is why we suggest a Mentoring Mesh. The mesh is made up of a number of individuals rather than just one, all of whom can impart you with knowledge, contacts, opportunities or whatever it is you may need as you are transitioning. It is not intended to replace a formal mentoring relationship but rather, it allows you to tap into the grey matter and experience of individuals who may have had a little more experience or knowledge of the industry or areas that you are looking to move into. Now, we are not suggesting having 10 mentors who you speak to for an hour every month say - that would be unsustainable. Rather, the mesh works like a board of advisors - it is a cohort you turn to, just like a company would, when they are seeking advice. Some of these people will become life long friends benefitting one another along the way.

## Establishing Your Mentoring Mesh

Exercise: Bring out your five-year fantasy goal - your aspirations for if you had no barriers whatsoever and owned a golden wand - and write down the overall objective of the fantasy. Underneath that, write down the tangible short-term steps that you need to take in order to achieve that long-term objective. List as many steps as possible as they will help you to identify the types of individuals who can aid your career or life transition.

Imagine you are looking to get a new job in a new industry or company; do you need introductions, sponsors, people who are going to give you potential projects? What new experience might you need? What support network could offer you that experience? Who knows you well enough to provide feedback or support?

At this point, we encourage LinkedIn to start becoming your new best friend. It is a great way of reconnecting with those individuals who you haven't necessarily liaised with in the last few years or whom you have been involved with from afar. Look to those individuals who may have been instructive at some point but who you may not have necessarily held close relationships with. Think outside of your normal circle of influence.

When Christina went from retail into consulting, she needed to develop her digital experience. She went about reading a variety of books and gathering information from virtual courses. One of her key supporters was, and still is, the woman who gave Christina her first consulting and training project in a company called Accenture after she lost her retail business. She acted as an informal mentor; Christina touches base with her every so often for advice. Christina knew she needed more support, so she also established informal mentoring relationships with an experienced trainer and consultant who gave her advice, case studies and ideas relating to specific projects. Nicola, her co-author, also served as Christina's sounding board in this new transition, which is how they both eventually set off to write their first book.

Nicola maintained relationships with people from her own network in Finance that enabled her to start her new business in Bristol: one of her friends from banking had started a property finance company, and the other had become a key advisor and CFO. They both agreed to invest in The Orange Tree Hub which was a startup co-working space with flats above.  When she was looking for work in a new city, Nicola reached out to friends in the finance industry and arranged to have a coffee with a local CEO of an insurance company who became a key mentor for her in her new city. It is not always the first person in the chain who is going to help you, but being open to discussions and becoming known as someone who steps up and helps others will always hold you in good stead.

Imagine you are trying to get a new position in a sales organization for another company. You know individuals in different industries and companies who could potentially help you. Let's take four of these individuals. The first is a Line Manager who you used to work with; they provide you with additional visibility for the project that you're interested in putting yourself forward for. They give you a testimonial on LinkedIn, saying that you are fantastic to work with and they would highly recommend you for projects. The second is a Director of Sales you know, they could be in a different company or industry altogether. They provide you with skills, experience and advice. You ask them directly, 'how do you sell in the time of Covid-19 when you can't actually go out and meet the customer?'. The third is the Director of Strategic

Partnerships. Again, this is a role that could be inside or outside your company. You tell them you're looking to move into the sales organization, and you ask them, 'Would you possibly know anyone who I could speak to relating to this role?'. The fourth is the Senior Director in a different company; they give you feedback based on industry trends and opportunities that are available.

As we've established, there's different things that we need from different people. The use of a mentoring mesh is an active and ongoing thing, it changes as our career and life aspirations change. Your mentoring mesh is dynamic, and the individuals you have on your mesh may not necessarily stay the same as you develop in your aspirations and your support-needs alter.

CREATING YOUR MENTORING MESH

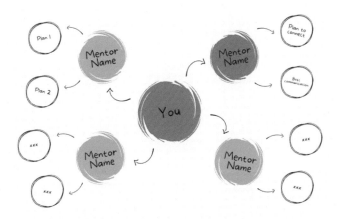

It's time to create your own mentoring mesh. Let's try a visual technique. Draw a circle in the middle of a big sheet of paper and write your name in the middle. Now, keeping your goals in mind, write down the names of the people that you think are going to be relevant to you. These may be individuals you already have in your network or they may hold influence in the industries that you're looking to move into. If you don't yet know the name, just write down the title or industry of the individual. At this point, please do not be limited as to whether you have access to them or not. However, it may not be realistic to write names such as Jeff Bezos or Richard Branson.  You might not be able to get to Bezos and Branson just yet, but there may be other entrepreneurs in the e-commerce world that are closer to home. We hope that you find excitement in this task and that it reveals that there is a universe of individuals that you could potentially approach for guidance and opportunities.

Let's use the individual who wanted to be the Chief Commercial Officer for a health tech as an example. She listed all the start-ups in health technology and she chose the companies that were of particular interest to her.  She then identified the job titles of the individuals she would need to be in touch with in order to obtain the guidance and advice that she was after.

Now, list the names of the individuals you would have in your mentoring mesh for your personal or professional aspirations and then pick 5 to 8 individuals who you would have as your personal board of directors. Imagine that you are in a big board room and that you could have those people around the table to give you advice in relation to your career journey. Write them and their job titles down.

STRATEGIES FOR APPROACHING MENTORS

## Making Yourself Relevant

Remember that your objective is to have these 8 individuals take time out of their very busy lives to offer you advice on an informal basis. You therefore need to identify why you would be relevant to them, why they should spend their precious time with you  (this is especially true if they don't know you very well). Be prepared for rejection, not everyone is going to say yes.

The approaching strategy we have devised is about being very careful in positioning yourself to potential mentors. Most importantly, you need to show relevance to them. By making yourself relevant, you're helping them to hone in on a topic that they may benefit from revisiting, creating a win-win scenario. Therefore, make sure you take the time to explore their area of expertise, what they write about on LinkedIn, what they post on YouTube or Twitter about, as these will most likely be the things they are interested in. Show a curiosity in these areas - they will hopefully be delighted to hear from someone who's been vocal about these particular topics too!

## Showing Interest....

There is nothing more powerful than complimenting someone... so the first thing to do when considering approaching a mentor is to think of how you can compliment them on their work, and how it has impacted you personally.

The second thing to do is to show interest in engaging with them in a conversation about what they are an authority in. You might approach an individual and say, 'I'm really interested in your industry and area of expertise, but I'd like to pick your brains on something particular. I hope I may be able to have 10 minutes of your time?' In this statement, you're making it quite clear that you're not going to ask for something too time-consuming (as time is the most precious of resources!). You are also stating that you are interested in their area of expertise and the conversation would be relevant to them.

If you are interested in an area of expertise, for example project management, demonstrate that you're interested in discussing the latest developments in that sector which only they can provide. We implore you to never just approach a potential mentor with 'I want you to be my mentor because I think you rock'; this is just too forward and very off-putting, especially if they don't know you!

Think about the kinds of people you could really learn from. What are the names of the individuals you want in your mentoring mesh? How can you make yourself relevant to them? Do you have 'extra curricular' interests in common such as golf or opera?

In our experience mentoring relationships usually come about as a result of a shared interest, or from working on a project. Nicola has several mentoring relationships through her rowing alumni network. She also has a long standing friend and mentor from her days at Citigroup whom she met when suggesting to her managers that she run an Emerging Markets Conference. The conference was initiated in order to help customers understand the rapidly changing landscape in the major Emerging Market countries. Senior managers were invited from the countries in question to meet a key group of clients who also had business in those countries. Emily was the Chief of Staff to the Emerging Markets at the time, and when Nicola approached her to help with the conference she was very willing to do so and brought in several senior participants. They worked together on the project and Nicola stayed in touch with Emily through email, coffees and lunches. In the end, Nicola took over Emily's role as Chief of Staff to the Emerging Markets when Emily left to head up a big charity project. They still connect today, over 15 years and several business ventures later.

What kind of person would you honestly have fun chatting to and spending time with? Mentoring is a two-way street and you ideally need to get along well with the person, otherwise it can be stilted. If you don't have opportunities to connect with senior people in your day to day life, start joining things so that you do gain exposure; volunteer to lead something like the Emerging Markets conference, go on a Habitat for Humanity day with your work, join a tennis club or go on an industry conference or self-development seminar where you may have a chance to meet senior people from other places. One of Nicola's entrepreneurial friends started his own 'Met Walking' networking group in Bristol where people simply go for a walk somewhere pretty and network there; it has some 150 members already.

BUILDING YOUR PERSONAl VISIBILITY PLAN

Once you have completed your list and written how you're going to be relevant to each individual, we will move on to thinking about how you can access these people. Nicola has shown some of her personal examples above. Be creative; cold calling isn't likely to find you a high quality mentoring relationship. We will explore the mentoring visibility channels that you can go on to use. In becoming visible to your potential mentors, we are inviting you to become very active on LinkedIn or other social media relevant to your industry or sector. There are new platforms emerging all the time; for example, Clubhouse is a platform used by lots of entrepreneurs where you can join a discussion being run by a key person and ask to speak.

It really helps to be heard at the same time as building your personal board of advisors. If there is a topic that you know your potential mentors are thought leaders in, build your voice around that subject. For example, if you're well known for customer experience and you want to get to a guru in customer experience that has a large role in a corporation, it helps if they can see that you are someone who has an opinion about the subject. In the same way you would at work, we encourage you to send any progress reports regarding your projects to those individuals who could be instructive in your next role or aspiration so they are aware of the great things you're doing. You can also go and speak at conferences to get your voice out there. Create blogs, write articles, launch a podcast. Use any opportunity to get your voice out. The more your voice is active and well-known, the more likely those individuals you approach will be willing to engage with you.

It's also important to build your contacts. There are interest groups that you can find on LinkedIn or outside of LinkedIn, e.g. customer experience or project management groups, in order to connect with others. Look to your friends, acquaintances or any other individuals in your network who could introduce you to relevant people. Search Alumni groups; who might you know in those groups who could potentially be a connector to someone else? You could even start your own club or networking group! Invite people into your circle who you believe are thought leaders in your sector or area of interest.

## Exercise: Create Your Personal Visibility Plan

This leads us on to the last exercise of the chapter - Your Personal Visibility Plan. Based on these ideas and examples, come up with ways that you can make yourself more visible to your potential board of advisors. Be creative and start building a picture of how you're going to get yourself out there. Which channels are most likely to be successful for you?

These exercises may take some time to crystalise, especially as you are formulating your new future. As with all the previous exercises in this book, these are part of your voyage of discovery of what is important for your future, so please don't rush it! Be strategic, focused and, most importantly, persevere! As you transform, a new world awaits and this is the way to get the support you need to Reconquer. It takes time to build your 'village' and to succeed - so invest the time in creating your Mentoring Mesh for success, and you will reap the benefits in the long-term.

---

**BOX 12: MENTORING AND VISIBILITY EXERCISE**

Create Your MentoringMesh

Define your MentoringMesh and how you will make yourself relevant to them

Devise your Personal Visibility Plan – how will you find those individuals and create a voice for yourself in your area of interest?

---

# CHAPTER 10
# OVERCOMING FEAR...
# TO RECONQUER

*'Each of us must confront our own fears, must come face to face with them. How we handle our fears will determine where we go with the rest of our lives. To experience adventure or to be limited by the fear of it.'* Judy Blume

## Rebooting for the Future

In this chapter, we are going to spend some time discussing one of the most important topics for those facing transformation - fear.

Fear will undoubtedly come up during any career transition or any type of change for that matter. Why? When you are faced with uncertainty, your brain's 'response centre' instructs your hormonal centre, the hypothalamus, to secrete cortisol, the stress hormone, and adrenaline, the action hormone. You may have heard of the notions of 'fight, flight, freeze'. When we feel fear, we experience exactly that. Your body is ready to either fight your threat, run from it, or freeze like a statue in the hope you are not noticed by your prey.

In order to overcome fear, your conscious mind needs to take over. In order to do this, we need to redefine it and learn to work alongside it. There has been a great deal written on this subject, especially in the Leadership and Entrepreneurial areas because leaders and entrepreneurs are constantly pushing the boundaries of the unknown. Fear is overcome with courage, which is not the absence of fear, but the *ability to take action in the presence of fear*. Courage comes from certainty and confidence, which are born out of consistency and trust, both in yourself and others. We've written about how we can become more certain in understanding our abilities, and having the confidence to trust ourselves.

In this chapter, we will look at some strategies to maximise fear's energy and potential, turning it into appropriate courageous action, while minimising the experience of fight, flight or freeze responses and any damage to your longer-term health from excess cortisol. We will also work on a fear antidote - your Personal Inspirations Pack.

Let's return to Christina's story. When she was going from her second redundancy to the potential launch of her new business - a bespoke retail jewelry concept - she had real misgivings on starting the business. As a corporate professional, she had never imagined that she could be an entrepreneur and was terrified by the very concept of it. She had a constant knot in her stomach; she was doubting that she could succeed, that she had the necessary knowledge. She would constantly question herself, 'Should I do this?', 'Should I not?'. Anxious scenarios would arise in her mind: 'What happens if it doesn't work?', 'What happens if I make big mistakes?', 'What if I get the shop in the wrong location?', 'What will my parents say if I fail?', 'What will the people I've worked with think of me?'. There was a whole range of negative possibilities in her head, spiraling out of control and holding her back. And the questions continued: 'What do I know about jewelry... About running a shop... About selling directly to customers? ...Selling online?'. She felt like everything was working against her.

REDEFINING F-E-A-R

When Jack Canfield talks about fear in his book *Chicken Soup for the Soul,* he uses the definition psychologists use: F-E-A-R as, 'Fantasized Experiences Appearing Real'. Because fear is all about what MIGHT happen – not what WILL happen.[15]

---

[15] Source: https://www.jackcanfield.com/blog/overcoming-fear

Fear is in the mind, it is a form of self-doubt, appearing as negative scenarios or 'what ifs'. Fear arises because we are creatures of comfort; we like to be in a space that we know and can control. Therefore, when we move into a new space we can feel out of control and in the dark. In Christina's case, she feared she couldn't control or understand the new retail sphere she was moving into.

Take Jack Canfield's re-definition of fear and recognise that fear is all in your head and in chemicals being produced to prepare you for a challenge. It is not reality. Yes, things can go wrong and things may not always go your way, but you have to remember that you are taking on your next venture because of your skill-set, knowledge and what you have to offer. Hopefully, your established BrandYou 2.0 has helped you to identify those great things you bring to the table in doing so!

You can take control of your fear by finding ways of reviewing and reshaping these fantasized experiences that are appearing real. To help you get there, let's do an exercise. Think about moments when you feel fear around an action you are considering. What do you experience in these moments? What are you saying to yourself? What language are you using?

You're probably using 'what if' language: 'what if it goes wrong...what if it doesn't work...what if I can't find the staff...what if it's the wrong company... what if I don't get the salary I want?' and so on. Your mind will come up with all sorts of reasons why something may not be the ideal. These are blockers - they are things that are preventing you from moving forward. To succeed, we must move beyond such blockers.

Nicola has a friend and mindset coach called Clare Doré. Clare runs an incredible group called Wild Women in

_____

Business and she frequently speaks on stage. She famously begins her talks by apologising in advance in case she breaks wind on stage (she uses a ruder word!). This always makes the audience howl with laughter and it's a good ice breaker, but there is a serious reason for her doing this. Having done the 'worst case scenario' exercise, she came up with this being one of the worst things that could happen, so she put it out there as if it was something that might actually happen, and the reality is obviously that it really isn't that bad!

## YOUR MOMENTS OF INVINCIBILITY

We doubt that there is any person on this planet who hasn't had to fight or put in effort to achieve something. We therefore know that you have overcome challenges in the past to achieve amazing things. Turn here to your Life Achievements Graph and see those achievements for yourself. Those are moments when you have been focused, resourceful and invincible. Tell yourself that you are great, that you have achieved things. However small our achievements may be (or seem to be) they are moments when we have felt and been strong. Realise that strength in you; it will take you onward and upwards. It's really important to not compare yourself to others, we have to be realistic to our environment and who we are.

Now that you know when you feel fear, let's do another exercise to find the moments you have felt truly invincible. When have you felt like Usain Bolt winning the 100 metres? Perhaps it was when you got your first job or gave in a paper that you thought you would never be able to get your head around.

Let's turn to an example from Christina. When she was at University in England, she chose to take up rowing, thinking of the most quintessentially British sport she could undertake. It was during a race in Bath, along a two mile stretch of the river Avon, that she felt totally invincible. While Christina and her team did not win the race, her elation was beyond anything she has felt since. Christina was ecstatic, on top of the world, adrenaline coursing through her body. On that day, after that race, whatever it was you asked Christina to do, she would have told you she could do it. Rowing gave her an opportunity to feel like she could take on the world. Nicola has had that feeling many times in a rowing boat and says that it's one of the most addictive things about rowing! The point is, this feeling can be replicated in other areas of life and once you have had it, you want more.

Use the table below. We invite you to write down a minimum of five moments like this. These don't just have to be professional; they could be hobbies or other personal achievements. Whatever it might be, these moments are important to you and they are a reminder of your internal strength.

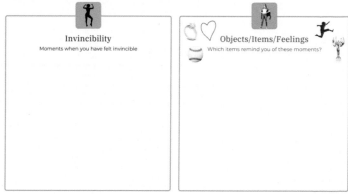

**Building Invincibility**

Invincibility
Moments when you have felt invincible

Objects/Items/Feelings
Which items remind you of these moments?

Now whenever you feel those pangs of fear, consciously think of those moments of invincibility. You can replace negative energy (after all, those butterflies in your stomach are all just energy, even if it is negative energy) with the positive energy associated with those Moments of Invincibility. This will help you reframe that fear into a positive outlet of energy.

THE FEAR ANTIDOTE: YOUR PERSONAL INSPIRATIONS PACK

To turn these Moments of Invincibility into even more powerful ammunition, we invite you to create your Personal Inspirations Pack. So, think about what artifact, item or feeling reminds you of that moment when you were invincible? Do you have a photo, a stub from an event, a quote, a certificate maybe? For example, Christina keeps a picture of the team in the rowing club as a reminder of her powerful moment. We invite you to pull all those items together, the artifacts and mementos, and create a personal inspiration pack. This could be physical, virtual or mental. In the case of the former, you may want to keep it about your person, in your wallet or in your handbag.

The powerful thing behind this strategy of the Personal Inspirations Pack is that you can refer to this collection at any time that you're feeling self-doubt or those Fantasized-Experiences-Appearing-Real. In doing so, you will be able to counteract fear, that negative voice in your head because you have done something amazing in the past and here is the evidence of it! The memory of that feeling of invincibility and power is a reminder that these traits are strong inside you. Harness that energy and push forward. This is a tried and tested way to build strength and invincibility. The foundation of overcoming anything is having the tools to overcome the feeling of F-E-A-R.

No matter what point in your life you are in, any point of inflection which is fueling your transformation is likely to be mired with moments where fear will petrify you. Recognise that this is absolutely normal. In our work with hundreds of professionals, using the strategies of the Moments of Invincibility and building a Personal Inspirations Pack have helped reframe stifling, paralysing F-E-A-R into positive energy, and, ultimately, positive action.

---

**BOX 13: PERSONAL INSPIRATIONS PACK**

Complete the exercises in this chapter:

When do you feel fear?

When do you / have you felt Invincible?

Create your Personal Inspirations Pack with all the artifacts, photos etc which remind you of those moments of invincibility.

When you have completed the above, how do you feel about the future moments when fear may come knocking on your door?

---

## CHAPTER 11
## BEING THE REPEAT
## RE-CONQUEROR

*'The responsibility of the leader is to think about the future no one else can.'* Peter Drucker

## Becoming The Repeat Re-Conqueror

Transformational Leadership has become a hot term in the last few years. What does it mean? According to leadership experts Bass and Rigio, *'Transformational leaders...are those who stimulate and inspire followers to both achieve extraordinary outcomes and, in the process, develop their own leadership capacity. Transformational leaders help followers grow and develop into leaders by responding to individual followers' needs by empowering them and by aligning the objectives and goals of the individual followers, the leader, the group, and the larger organization.'*[16]

According to Bass, transformational leadership can be defined based on the impact that it has on followers. Transformational leaders, Bass suggested, garner trust, respect, and admiration from their followers. The reason? Transformational leaders believe that their followers can do their best, leading members of the group to feel inspired and empowered.[17]

---

[16] Source: https://www.verywellmind.com/what-is-transformational-leadership-2795313

[17] Source: https://www.verywellmind.com/what-is-transformational-leadership-2795313

We wholeheartedly embrace this definition of Transformational Leadership. We would, however, add one more dimension. The ability to embrace change and inspire change in others on an on-going basis. Covid-19 has shown us that it is important to be able to hone in on the skill set of living, and thriving, through constant re-invention.

Now, more than ever, we are entering a phase in business and beyond where uncertainty will constantly prevail. Future pandemics, climate change and wars are likely to become more common. These will constantly test us as individuals, as companies, as communities.

As we find ourselves thrown into the waves of constant change, we will have to sharpen our skillset of coping with, adapting to, and thriving in change. We expect that when we have achieved our objectives or reached the goal we had set for ourselves, that is the end of the journey. The reality is that when we reach our goal, a new destination is set in our minds. This is likely to already have happened to you - how many times have you been involved in a project where success may have been achieved, only to find out the next day that the goalposts have moved and a new objective has been set by your organisation? Or in the context of our simple fitness journey, once we achieve our ideal fitness level, we then have to work to maintain it or, even, improve it. The transformation continues. The beauty of going through the steps we have just gone through is that they are relevant to pivots and transitions whatever the context. The power that goes with regaining control of your life, your environment, or your business imbues you with an internal strength to Reconquer repeatedly.

How do you create this ability?

- Create your Tribe

- Become a Transformational Mentor... for others

- Encourage intergenerational adaptability

CREATE YOUR TRIBE - BEHIND YOUR MOVEMENT

*'Goals are about the results you want to achieve. Systems are about the processes that lead to those results.'* James Clear

In his book *Atomic Habits*, James Clear talks about the importance of distinct habits to encourage long-term, successful change. He sets out a thesis that for change to happen, we have to not only set goals but, more importantly, assimilate behaviours, habits, which will lead us to our desired results.

He states *'One of the most effective things you can do to build better habits is to join a culture where (1) your desired behaviour is normal behaviour and (2) you already have something in common with the group'*[18]

He recounts the story of the Polgar sisters - 3 Hungarian girls who became chess prodigies. Their home 'culture' was that of a space dedicated to chess and competitions - the sisters played against each other, against their parents, and they participated in every chess competition they could enter. The youngest sister, Judit, became the youngest grand master of all time aged 15 years and 4 months old (younger than Bobby Fischer, the previous record holder).

It is in harnessing the habits which are the most attractive and making those behaviours your 'normal' and creating a culture around you to maintain this new normal which

---

[18] Source: Atomic Habits, James Clear. Page 122

will keep you moving forward.

*'We are what we repeatedly do. Excellence, therefore, is not an act but a habit'* Aristotle

As a leader, we encourage you to take this one step further - to take the reins and create your own 'tribe' or community where transformation is embraced and encouraged. Take the opportunity to build an army of transformation champions around you. You will find that you will actively seek out others who want to make change in their life, business or work, and your tribe will grow. You will benefit from the positive energy of those who have been on a similar journey with you or, in the best of cases, you will become that driver of change for others. This is where you are the builder of a 'chameleonic culture', a culture in a business or group where you aspire to, and are able to, drive transformation.

It is not enough for us to talk about transformation or change. It is important to enthuse others, drive change, and harness the power of creating a movement. Don't waste the opportunity of having worked so hard to not share the chance for others to grow and flourish. Become that role-model for those around you, your family, your colleagues, your friends. Use your new-found energy and innate strength to rally those around you and work with them through the skills and techniques we have outlined in this book.

## How do you start?

Think of the area you have worked on for your transformation. Is it personal - e.g. weight loss? Business related - e.g. embedding a new digital system? Or in your home life – e.g. working on a relationship?

Review your BrandYou 2.0 - what community would underline the YOU you would like to be associated with?

An example is Christina's most recent personal transformation - she turned herself from an overweight, depressive, chronic disease sufferer whose hormones controlled her, to a 15-kilos lighter, healthy super-fit perimenopausal woman. As a result she created the "Midlife Reboot Tribe' encouraging women in midlife to take control of their bodies and minds.

Give your community a name and invite like-minded individuals to join it. Encourage conversation and knowledge sharing. Facebook and Linked-In make it so easy to do this today!

## BECOME A TRANSFORMATIONAL MENTOR

Research shows that the best way to learn is to teach others. By creating your Tribe, you are building a wider network as a support group, a group of inspiration. That is powerful, yet the greatest depth of learning will come with the ability to mentor others.

Mentoring, the development of longer- term relationships with peers or colleagues, allows for deeper interactions and 2-way conversations which will continue to inspire you to sharpen your transformation skills while also encouraging others to take on their own transitions.

If you are in business, seek out those people, teams or departments that have been resistant to change. If you are on your personal or career transformation, embrace mentees who you know are aiming to change. As the authors of this book, we implore that you look around you now and take note of at least three people who you can help start or reignite their transformation projects.

Act as a mentor, a guide, a supporter for others. If a formal mentoring relationship may seem daunting for you, then take charge by becoming an informal mentor to others. Encourage them to create their Mentoring Mesh, and be one of the informal mentors in their Mesh!

If there is one thing that Covid-19 has demonstrated to the world, it is that we cannot act alone and we need to support others. Transformation is hard and is mired by obstacles and negative self-talk. This is where you come in; as a transformational leader, you are now able to be compassionate and empathize with others who may be struggling with seeking a new path or adapting to change.

You can take your mentees through the systems and processes we have outlined in this book, enabling you to drive further change and, deepen your personal commitment to inspiring that change.

HARNESSING YOUTH - CATALYSTS FOR TRANSFORMATION

One of the greatest shifts that we will see in the world is the rise of Generation Z. This generation, born in the early 2000s, are now entering the workforce and are a generation guided by innate adaptability. This generation grew up with social media and have a talent for absorbing information and new ways of thinking which Baby Boomers and Millenials have not developed to the same extent. Generation Z is a generation hungry for change.

According to the research from Ernst and Young Generation Z are *'a generation that is more independent than the generation it follows, and endlessly empowered. At the same time, its members are negotiating life without the guard rails past generations have known. Through it all, they are changing society, redefining cultural norms established by their predecessors.'[19]*

So, if you are working in business (or even if you have a family with teenagers) we encourage you to use your renewed skills for transformation in creating a work /

---

[19] Source: https://www.ey.com/en_us/consulting/how-contradictions-define-generation-z.

home environment that embraces change by creating what we call a 'chameleonic culture'. As Generation Z come into, and up, the ranks, companies will be wise to harness their empowered attitude and willingness to shape a world which is inclusive, equitable and socially responsible, elements which Generation Z value highly[20].

By informally mentoring others, especially the younger generation, you will be actively creating a culture of inclusiveness and cross-fertilisation of ideas. The Microsoft survey which coined the Great Resignation demonstrated that, *'individuals with strong workplace networks and [who] feel included at work were reported to be the most productive and innovative'.* On the contrary, *'those who reported weaker workplace relationships were less likely to report thriving at activities that lead to innovation, like thinking strategically, collaborating or brainstorming with others and proposing new ideas'.*

We cannot stress enough the importance of using inter-generational agility in encouraging high-performance and productivity in every area of life. By allowing yourself to listen to, consider and act on the ideas of the younger generation, you will be tapping into the most creative sources of innovation to do so. In a 2020 Harris Poll study, Generation Z considers itself naturally creative - 56% considered themselves creative, compared to 44% of those over the age of 24.[21]

Don't waste another second: strengthen your ability to Reboot, Rebuild, Reconquer™ by helping those in your circle of influence do just that. In a post-pandemic reality, this is just an imperative.

---

[20] Source: https://www.ey.com/en_us/consulting/how-contradictions-define-generation-z

[21] Source: https://eu.usatoday.com/story/news/nation/2020/08/18/generation-z-may-most-creative-yet-study-says/5589601002/)

---

**BOX 14: TO HELP OTHERS**

Set up your Tribe in your area of interest - your community of like-minded people to exchange ideas and support.

Identify 2 people who you want to become an informal Mentor to - they may be your peer or, friends; pick people who you know are aiming to make changes in their life, work or community and guide them through the process (you can use the resources in this book!)

Encourage intergenerational adaptability - seek to informally mentor at least 2 Gen Z individuals. Learn from them on what they seek to change and see how you can best support them.

---

*'Men are born soft and supple; dead they are stiff and hard.*

*Plants are born tender and pliant; dead, they are brittle and dry.*

*Thus whoever is stiff and inflexible is a disciple of death.*

*Whoever is soft and yielding is a disciple of life.*

*The hard and stiff will be broken.*

*The soft and supple will prevail.'* Lao Tzu

Well done on completing your Reboot! You are all set to finalise your Rebuild and set off to Reconquer! We would love to hear your stories of transformation.  You can share them with us online at rebootmylife.guide

BS - #0003 - 090123 - C136 - 216/138/9 - PB - 9780956766649 - Matt Lamination